Walking with Henry is a breath of fresh air. Each page is filled with golden nuggets of wisdom that unexpectedly drop into your hand and heart like little gifts wrapped in packages of well-crafted words. If you've been looking for a read to snuggle up with, cry with, laugh with, and ultimately grow with—this is it. Rachel Anne Ridge writes the way she lives: full of grace, contagious joy, and a wide-open heart. That's why I know you'll enjoy this book as much as I have.

PRISCILLA SHIRER, Bible teacher and author

This tender book will pull you into Rachel's and Henry's stories and lift you up to Jesus. I love this book!

SHEILA WALSH, author of *It's Okay Not to Be Okay*

Who knew there are so many lessons about faith, grace, and letting go of past regrets that you can learn from a miniature donkey named Henry? *Walking with Henry* is the beautifully written story of two donkeys who had to find their way and let go of fear as they forged a relationship they weren't sure they even wanted. You'll laugh, you'll cry, and most of all, you'll never forget the impact the humblest of creatures can have on the way you view your faith and your God. Rachel Anne Ridge has written another heartwarming book that will charm you and challenge you in all the best ways.

MELANIE SHANKLE, *New York Times* bestselling author and speaker

Personal, reflective, practical, and profound, *Walking with Henry* shows us how the Lord can provide timely, beautiful wisdom from an unlikely and unexpected teacher. Rachel Anne's words are thought provoking and life giving, the very best kind of medicine for a weary soul.

SOPHIE HUDSON, author of *Giddy Up, Eunice* and cohost of *The Big Boo Cast*

A five-star read! Rachel is all heart . . . and wait until you meet Henry. Who will want this book? People who (1) love animals, (2) dream about farm life, (3) want to deepen their prayer lives, (4) have ever felt guilty, and (5) have a pulse!

PATSY CLAIRMONT, speaker and author of *You Are More Than You Know*

I'm not much of an animal person, which is why I am amazed at Rachel's ability to make me love *two* donkeys. This book is a thoroughly enjoyable reminder to be actively aware of the many ways God seeks to use the normal moments of life to teach us.

EMILY THOMAS, *The Struggle Well Project* podcast

When I first read *Flash*, I fell in love with Rachel's world. Never did I think the same magic could happen again! Yet *Walking with Henry* is filled with wit, grace, and beautiful lessons as we watch Rachel and her donkey friends live the life God has given them.

LISA WHELCHEL, actress, author, speaker, and life coach

Rachel Anne Ridge has a unique and endearing gift of finding spiritual wisdom in unusual places. A rescued miniature donkey with lots of behavioral baggage arrives during a time of deep personal searching in Rachel's life. Her journey with Henry is a sweet and vulnerable story that will make you smile, think deeply, and ultimately worship our Creator God.

DAVE BURCHETT, author of *Stay: Lessons My Dogs Taught Me about Life, Loss, and Grace*

walking with henry

RACHEL ANNE RIDGE

walking with
henry

*Big Lessons from a Little Donkey
on Faith, Friendship, and
Finding Your Path*

TYNDALE
MOMENTUM®

*The nonfiction imprint of
Tyndale House Publishers, Inc.*

242
Ridge

For Tom,
my companion
and the love of my life.

Contents

An Invitation   *xi*

Prologue   *xv*

Chapter 1   **The Means of Grace**   *1*
Daily Morning Prayer and
Daily Evening Prayer:
Rite Two, "The General Thanksgiving"

Chapter 2   **I Believe**   *13*
Daily Morning Prayer and
Daily Evening Prayer:
Rite Two, "The Apostles' Creed"

Chapter 3   **All That I Need**   *31*
Psalm 23

Chapter 4   **Open Our Eyes**   *49*
Prayers for the World:
"For Joy in God's Creation"

Chapter 5   **What We've Left Undone**   *63*
Daily Morning and Evening Prayer:
Rite Two, "Confession of Sin"

Chapter 6   **This New Day**   *81*
Daily Morning Prayer:
Rite Two, "A Collect for Grace"

Chapter 7   **People of His Pasture**   *95*
Daily Morning Prayer:
Rite Two, "Venite: Psalm 95:1-7"

Chapter 8   Lead Us Not   113
              The Lord's Prayer

Chapter 9   Infected Hearts   133
              Prayers for the World:
              "For the Human Family"

Chapter 10   O Gracious Light   155
              Order for Evening:
              Rite Two, "O Gracious Light
              (Phos hilaron)"

Chapter 11   The Way of Peace   169
              Daily Morning Prayer:
              Rite Two, from "The Song of Zechariah
              (Benedictus Dominus Deus): Luke 1:68-79"

Chapter 12   Companion in the Way   181
              Daily Evening Prayer:
              Rite Two, "A Collect for the Presence of Christ"

Chapter 13   Glory Be   197
              Daily Morning Prayer and
              Daily Evening Prayer:
              Rite One, "Gloria"

              Your Guide to Prayer Walking   213
              Acknowledgments   219
              Notes   223
              Resources   229
              About the Author
              (and Her Donkeys)   233

An Invitation

"It's okay, little donkey," I murmured, my voice low and reassuring. "It's okay."

I stood at the pasture gate, a small blue halter in hand and a braided lead rope looped around my arm. This long-awaited day was finally here, and anticipation fluttered in my chest. The buckles jangled as I pulled off the price tag that still dangled from the nylon nose strap. I knew the halter, made for a pony, wouldn't fit properly on my new miniature donkey—a little too snug over the top of his head and too loose across the nose—but it would do for now.

Today's lesson would be short. He needed to get used to me and become familiar with being handled and led. Henry was a rescue animal: a stray with an unknown past who was clearly uncertain about his present. I patted my pocket for the carrots I'd brought as a treat, then lifted the heavy chain link off the rusty nail sticking out of the fence post. Oversized ears swung in my direction as he listened to my cautious approach.

"It's okay, little donkey," I repeated, like a chant now. "It's okay." As the words hung suspended between us, I realized these were words I longed to hear myself.

Will I be okay too? My heart wanted to know.

So much had happened to bring me to this day—and to this donkey. I swallowed hard and fought back a tear that puddled unexpectedly at the corner of my eye. Beneath my calming demeanor was a jumble of emotions: Regret. Sadness. Fear. Anxiety. Doubt. And . . . just a teeny bit of hope. Maybe somehow this small, dark chocolate–colored donkey could make everything all right again.

It was a big ask for such a little guy.

Though I didn't know it that morning in the pasture as I knelt next to this tiny rescue donkey, I was on the edge of a pilgrimage.

Not everyone gets a moment they can point back to as their starting place, and fewer still get a donkey to journey forward with. But I would walk with Henry. I would walk, and I would try to pray.

At least, that was my goal.

This pasture would become the perfect setting for facing the anxieties over my circumstances and the unexpected wrestling with my faith that had both come calling. Outside, in a wide-open field laced with footpaths, I would find space to breathe and be invited to let go of the fears that had brought my spiritual life to a standstill.

Walking with a donkey, as I learned, is not done with the purposeful strides of personal achievement, but rather with the humbled steps of one forced to go at the pace of an unhurried companion. Although I couldn't yet see it, ahead of me on the paths was a whole new dimension of finding God's presence, not only in His creation but also in the timeless prayers of the church—the voices of His people throughout the ages.

^ ^

In the pages of this book, I invite you to walk (or amble, or balk) with me. Trust me, it's a slow process, so you'll have no trouble keeping up. There is plenty of time to pause along the way if you need it.

You see, I had always expected to pinpoint my problems and quickly find solutions for them. I attempted to quell my doubts with well-chosen Bible verses. My bookshelves were lined with every version of "Simple Steps to a Fulfilled Life." I attended conferences and retreats, and I listened to sermons and motivational speakers. I put on the armor of God and fought the devil. I filled the holes in my spiritual life with activities and productive practices designed to make me grow as a Christian.

But beneath the busyness was a growing realization that something was missing. I longed for a sense of the sacred, for an uncluttered faith that was open to mystery and wonder.

I needed to do something different. I wanted stories to ponder and safe spaces to ask questions of God. Yet I had come to a place in which I no longer possessed the words to pray. *Maybe written prayers could help me*, I thought. Somehow, I knew that I must walk with a donkey, with a book of prayers in hand. An ambling pace, coupled with quiet contemplations, would be the perfect antidote for my hurried schedule and worried existence.

A donkey cares nothing about human time-management systems, believe me. He is not concerned with the opinions of others or what is trending on social media, or what your theology is. A donkey will, though, disarm you, make you smile, help you open the door to questions, and leave room for conversation. In fact, traveling with a donkey is like stepping back in time, sometimes right into the pages of the Bible and into the ancient traditions of prayer and meditation.

If you've found yourself in a situation like mine, maybe this will be a good place to start. Join me on a walk as we learn to let go, embrace a deeper faith, and find a way to the sacred. This path reminds us that life is a journey best traveled with a friend—one step at a time.

Prologue

F lash needed a wingman.

To be clear, in the seven years my husband, Tom, and I had owned him, Flash (in typical stoic donkey fashion) had never actually verbally complained about his solitary existence in our pasture. But I could see it in his stance, the droop of his head, and the shuffle of his feet—he was lonely out there all by himself. Obviously, he needed a donkey friend.

This would not be an easy sell to Tom. For the most part, he went along with my ideas. But acquiring a second donkey for the sake of the first donkey's mental state? That might be a bridge too far, even for him. In more than thirty years of marriage, we had honed the art of negotiation pretty well. I knew it would require several well-timed conversations to get the ball rolling in the right direction before going in for the closer. I thought carefully about how to frame the situation.

"Look how pitiful Flash looks out there," I said casually over my morning coffee.

Step One.

Tom glanced out the window at the large, shaggy animal who stood near the pasture gate just beyond our backyard. Flash's brownish-gray coat was beginning to shed with the warming spring season, giving him a particularly disheveled appearance. He swung his head low and jutted out his bottom lip, as if right on cue.

Good job, Flash.

"No, we aren't getting another donkey." Tom leaped past my carefully crafted plan and straight to the punch line.

Rats! He saw right through me. If only Lauren, Meghan, and Grayson were here.

Our three kids would have cast their votes with me, and we could have come up with a compelling argument for getting another donkey. But they were grown and gone now: Lauren and Meghan were both married, and Grayson had recently left home for college.

When Flash had first wandered onto our dirt driveway, we'd all given Tom our best pitches for keeping this stray donkey that no one else apparently wanted. In the end, Tom didn't need much persuading at all, for he had already fallen victim to the donkey's charms. Flash's fuzzy ears, his soft brown eyes, and his endearing expressions had made the decision easy, and we never regretted making him part of our family.

Well, maybe once, but probably not more than twice did we have second thoughts. Flash couldn't help that he was inquisitive and opinionated—and weighed five hundred pounds. It's just that those characteristics sometimes got him into trouble.

Tom looked at me and grinned. "Remember the time Flash broke into the tack room and ate an entire bucket of grain? He made such a mess in the barn, with no concern that his muddy hoofprints were evidence left at the crime scene."

"I thought he was going to be so sick!" I replied.

I could laugh about it now, but when Flash stumbled over a stump in the pasture not long afterward, I was convinced his gluttony had caused laminitis, a condition that potentially leads to lameness and even death. Fortunately, Flash seemed to have a stomach made of iron—aside from a major bout of flatulence, he was perfectly fine.

The truth of the matter was that even though Flash was technically "my" donkey, Tom was the one he truly adored. Tom had initially worked with Flash to help him overcome his fear of people and learn to trust us. Day after day, for hours at a time, Tom would sit in the pasture with Flash. The two of them had a special bond that transcended Tom's busy schedule and Flash's knack for nosing into trouble.

All negotiating games aside, I *was* worried about Flash. Donkeys are very social by nature; without another animal's company, preferably a donkey or horse, they simply don't thrive as well as they should. They can become depressed (an actual veterinary term), lose their appetite, become uninterested in their surroundings, and get sick. Lonely donkeys can become bored and destructive, chewing on fences and barns and anything lying around. Flash had begun to exhibit all these qualities.

"We do need to talk about this," I said. "You know that Flash still misses—"

"Yeah, he *is* getting worse," Tom interrupted before I could finish. He was going to keep things light for me. "He can't resist picking up and trying to break my ropes and extension cords.

He steps down on them and then yanks with his teeth. I can't leave anything out anymore."

He looked at me and gave me a wink. "Maybe we just need to get rid of Flash."

Tough talker. I slugged Tom's arm (he didn't even wince) and began making inquiries about companion donkeys.

^ ^

"I think I've found a good buddy for Flash," the private Facebook message from Doc Darlin said. Though his real name was David C. Duncan, he was known as "Doc Darlin" in the Concho Valley area of West Texas. The name suited him well. He was a burro wrangler who worked at a donkey rescue in San Angelo, Texas, where I had met him a year or so earlier while checking out the ranch as I researched information about donkey care. It's the main facility for Peaceful Valley Donkey Rescue, the largest organization of its kind in the United States, which serves to care for, train, and rehome thousands of animals.

When I parked the car that day, Doc was in the yard working with a shaggy brown donkey. It looked like Doc was training him to walk on a lead, and the donkey was having none of it. Front feet planted and head low, he refused to budge an inch. Doc eased up on the rope and bent over close to the animal's ears, whispering something I couldn't hear. The donkey cocked his head, seemed to think for a moment, and then stepped forward as if under Doc's magic spell. I was impressed.

Mark, the founder of the organization, introduced us. "Doc is our public liaison, so you'll likely be connecting with him in the future." Doc touched his fingertips to his cowboy hat and smiled through his mustache. I liked him immediately and began to fill him in on Flash's backstory.

Doc was fascinated with how Flash had come into my life, seemingly out of nowhere. When I told him our local sheriff had confessed he couldn't get five dollars for Flash at auction, Doc grimaced. He'd heard stories like that a hundred times over.

"And Flash's adventures on our small farm in Texas have become the inspiration for a book," I explained.

"Well, I'll be," Doc said, shaking his head in delight. "Don't that beat all."

Now, Doc's message stared at me from my computer screen, in response to the query I'd sent some weeks earlier. In my e-mail I'd reminded him about Flash and explained I was looking for a companion for him, preferably a miniature donkey who was used to being with other donkeys. I needed one that would be good at hanging out with Flash each day in the pasture, as well as accompanying him to public events so he wouldn't be nervous—not that Flash had been asked to any public events yet, but I was planning ahead just in case.

I didn't tell Doc the main reason Flash needed a companion now. I couldn't tell him about Flash's grief, or my own—at least not yet.

Doc's message continued: "This fella is a miniature, and he came to us as part of a group of twenty strays that were rounded up in Henderson County, Texas. The sheriff logged him in as 'Number Ten.' I've included a picture."

Well, one glance at Henderson County Stray Number Ten's sweet baby face in the photo, and I was a goner. Standing next to a standard-sized donkey, he looked tiny! At only thirty-six inches high at the shoulder, he seemed small enough to fit into a duffel bag! His stiff mane stood straight up along his neck, and his dark eyes seemed to gaze right into my heart. He was just what I was hoping for.

With a little more persuasion, Tom eventually warmed to the idea and was supportive, so we made arrangements to borrow a horse trailer from a friend of a friend. Tom would be the designated driver; we were hoping to make the ten-hour round-trip in one day, and I knew I couldn't do it without him. The trailer was enormous—large enough for two draft horses plus their tack—but when the day came, we hooked it up to our Suburban with a "beggars can't be choosers" shrug.

Rumbling down the highway at dawn, I turned to look at Tom. "I really want this new donkey to be a good friend for Flash," I said.

But what I actually meant was, *I want him to fix everything.*

Tom reached for my hand and gave it a squeeze. "It's gonna be fine. You'll see."

CHAPTER 1

The Means of Grace

Almighty God, Father of all mercies,
we your unworthy servants give you humble thanks
for all your goodness and loving-kindness to us and to all
whom you have made. We bless you for our creation,
preservation, and all the blessings of this life;
but above all for your immeasurable love
in the redemption of the world by our Lord Jesus Christ;
for the means of grace, and for the hope of glory.
And, we pray, give us such an awareness of your mercies,
that with truly thankful hearts we may show forth your praise,
not only with our lips, but in our lives, by giving up
our selves to your service, and by walking before you in holiness
and righteousness all our days; through Jesus Christ our Lord,
to whom, with you and the Holy Spirit,
be honor and glory throughout all ages. Amen.

Daily Morning Prayer and Daily Evening Prayer: Rite Two,
"The General Thanksgiving," *The Book of Common Prayer*

Will our new donkey enjoy his new home? The long westward highway flattened out ahead of us as we left the rolling hills and trees of north central Texas behind, giving me plenty of time to imagine his first impressions. *I hope he likes us.*

With the giddy anticipation of an adoptive pet-parent, I'd made sure his living area was tidy and ready for him: fresh water in a large bucket, holding pen free of sticks and debris, and hay set aside to be served. Although I knew he would only see the barn and pasture, in my nervous zeal I'd cleaned the entire house and breezeway, just in case he might want a tour. I mean, you never know . . .

It was Saturday, official chore day at the Ridge household. As I swept the concrete floor of the breezeway, I mentally clicked through the rest of the tasks on my to-do list. With only Tom and me at home, there were fewer messes to clean up and no one else to blame for all the shoes left out and dishes in the sink. A good chunk of that blame rested with yours truly. What can I say? I'm just a humble tool in the hands of the Lord for refining the patience of the neatnik whom I married.

I rested my chin on the top of the broom handle and thought back to a memorable chore day several years earlier, when Meghan and Grayson were still at home. I had barked out orders to clean up their toxic-waste-dump bedrooms or else, while I focused my attention on the main living areas.

Tom's task for the day was replacing the driver's seat belt on our (then) fifteen-year-old Explorer. I could tell his patience was at the breaking point when he came inside to get a drink of water and said preemptively, "Don't talk to me."

I had followed orders, continuing to move from room to room through the house. Checking on the kids' progress, I jabbed my pointer finger first at Meghan and then the vacuum before giving Grayson a look that communicated my wishes: *Put down the Legos and get to work. And no, I don't care if you're hungry right now.*

Suddenly, I heard a noise coming from outside and looked up to see Tom banging on the glass sliding door that leads from the breezeway into the house.

I couldn't believe my eyes. My husband's face was contorted, and he was covered in blood!

Dear God, he's been shot! Oh, Lord!

My mind raced in a thousand directions, but my body was frozen in place. I knew Tom would collapse any minute, from sheer blood loss alone.

I immediately commenced crying and praying and looking for my phone so I could dial 911. It had to have been a shotgun at point-blank range!

How is he still standing?

And then I heard . . .

"It's P-P-PAINT! I accidentally punctured a red spray can, and it exploded in the back seat! I can't see! It's in my nose and throat, and it's everywhere inside the truck!"

Not blood—just paint.

We sprang into action. While Tom hosed himself down and got somewhat cleaned up, Meghan, Grayson, and I grabbed rubber gloves and paint thinner. After madly ripping old towels into rags, we began wiping down the truck as quickly as we could. The back seat, the carpet, the backs of the front seats, and the ceiling were solid red, while the insides of the doors and windows wore a splattering of the quickly drying enamel.

We were like a CSI team cleaning up a gruesome crime scene, toiling for hours in the sweltering heat, not saying a word except for an occasional whispered request: "Pass the paint thinner, please."

Finally Meghan asked, "Does this kind of thing happen to other people too, or just us?"

There was a long pause as we all looked at one another. There we were—sweaty, greasy, covered with red paint, our rubber gloves dissolving at the fingertips like decaying flesh—feeling like the survivors of the French Revolution in *Les Misérables*. Oh, mercy. We were such a pitiful sight!

The question hung in the fume-filled air—until we began to laugh . . .

When we pulled ourselves together, I assured Meghan, "Oh, no, sweetheart. This kind of thing *only* happens to us."

We broke down in hysterics once again.

Just when we were feeling alone in our misery, a sparkling moment had been interjected.

I needed it just then.

So often I have felt alone in my particular trying circumstance.

Surely no one else drives a fifteen-year-old vehicle with a broken seat belt. No one else is forced to clean up paint explosions. No one else has struggled through failure and loss in the same ways I have. No one else has experienced *whatever it is* that I am going through.

Sometimes I just want to know: Am I the only one?

Because it *feels* like I am.

Then, when I least expect it, a small beam of light breaks through the darkness and offers a glimpse of goodness. A reminder, perhaps, that I am never *really* alone.

Grace is present.

And if grace is present, then God is too.

Doc met us as we pulled up, directing Tom to pull the horse trailer to a spot near one of the outbuildings. We got out of the truck and stretched our legs after the long drive, taking in the scene around us. Donkeys of every shape, color, and size roamed in pens and dry pastures in all directions. Big donkeys, little donkeys, donkeys with babies, old donkeys. Seeing more than a thousand donkeys in one place at one time is almost impossible to comprehend. It's noisy, and dusty, and utterly overwhelming.

I couldn't help it: I immediately thought of Abraham and his flocks of sheep and goats, his herds of cattle and donkeys described in the Bible. *Is this what his nomadic empire might have actually looked like?*

Suddenly more questions popped into my mind: *Where did they get water? What did the animals eat? How did Abraham's hired hands keep the animals from running off? What did they do with all the poop?* It must have been quite an operation!

"Howdy!" Doc shook our hands and introduced himself to Tom. Wearing a cowboy hat with a crumpled brim, a red bandana around his neck, and work-worn Western boots, Doc looked as if he had stepped out of the pages of a history book. We weren't the least bit surprised to learn he sometimes participates in 1800s-era historic reenactments. He could certainly carry off the part of a Civil War soldier or a Wild West cowboy.

"I know y'all are anxious to meet your new donkey, so let's go on over to where he's waitin' for ya," Doc said with a smile. "I'll let y'all get to know each other a bit, and then we'll head inside to fill out the paperwork."

We rounded the corner, and there he was: Henderson Number Ten. Freshly brushed and groomed, he was haltered on a lead rope and voraciously eating tufts of green grass in the yard. While I held out my hands for the donkey to smell, a volunteer named Margaret, who was holding his lead rope, told us what little the ranch knew about him.

"All we really know is that he was found wandering around Henderson County with a bunch of other donkeys. He was the only mini in the group, which means he probably knows how to hold his own. We don't think he's been handled a lot, but he has an engaging personality, and he's not afraid of people," she said, ruffling his ears. Margaret had the compassionate air of a true animal lover, and I could see she thought highly of this one.

The donkey ignored my outstretched hands in favor of the grass, so I knelt down next to him and began to stroke his neck. His dark summer coat was smooth and shiny, with an even darker "cross" marking on his shoulders. His stubby legs had faint stripes below the knees, and his tail swished flies rather futilely. Two soft ears twitched this way and that, letting me know that even though he seemed focused solely on his snack, he was paying attention to my voice and presence. He had a warm-gray muzzle that matched the light-colored circles around his eyes. In short, he was adorable.

I was smitten.

Doc jumped in. "We think he is about seven or eight years old, and he has a great disposition. Since he's used to being part of a herd, he's not going to have any problems socializing with Flash. In fact, he will probably really enjoy having one single friend."

"What's up with his stomach?" Tom asked.

"Yeah, he's pretty round," Doc laughed. "But that's perfectly normal. Minis don't have a whole lot of room for their organs and stomach, so they always look kinda fat."

Hey, now. That's my donkey you're talking about! I was already defensive.

Doc continued. "Since we knew he might be around a lot of people, we actually led him in a parade last weekend to see how he would do. He was fantastic! He just walked right along like he knew what he was doing. Didn't balk or anything!"

I swelled with pride. *My goodness, my donkey didn't balk in a parade!*

Not only that, but Henderson Number Ten also jumped up into the horse trailer like a professional after the adoption paperwork was done and we were ready to leave. The donkey looked ridiculously small inside the cavernous space, the soft tips of his brown ears just reaching the bottom of the window openings along the side of the trailer. Tom closed the door and secured it.

"Now, just a word of caution," Doc said. "When donkeys get nervous, they tend to have explosive diarrhea. Don't be alarmed if this happens. He's already been through who-knows-what, and he'll have to get used to lots of new things, including Flash." He gave the trailer a couple of taps and smiled. "On that note, good luck to y'all!"

Grace.

Right now, grace looked like a charming miniature donkey in a big old horse trailer making its way across Texas in the fading daylight. It looked like a chance to pick up some broken pieces and begin again.

An artist I admire has said,

> I have discovered that something is awakened through failure, tragedy, and disappointment. It is a place of learning and potential creativity. In such moments you can get lost in despair or denial, or you can recognize the failure and run toward the hope of something new.

I've experienced grace in a thousand ways in my life and missed it in a thousand more. Maybe it's because grace rarely arrives with fanfare and a parade. But somehow, it always comes. After all that we'd been through to bring us to Henderson Number Ten, I had hope that grace would come once again.

I leaned back into the passenger seat and adjusted the pillow in my lap. (Yes, I have a lap pillow to rest my arms on when I travel. Doesn't everyone?) As we chased our long shadow down the highway toward home, I pulled out a small red notebook and opened to the first pages. Inside, I'd copied a prayer that I wanted to memorize. To this day, "The General Thanksgiving," from *The Book of Common Prayer*, is my favorite, perhaps because it reminds me of that long drive home with our small passenger and my deep sense of gratitude. I stopped on these words and let them rest on my soul:

> *. . . for your immeasurable love in the redemption of the world by our Lord Jesus Christ; for the means of grace, and for the hope of glory.*

The means of grace.

One little donkey, out of a sea of a thousand donkeys, was traveling to a nice home tonight. He'd been chosen for a special job—hand selected to become part of our lives as a friend for Flash. I suppose you could call that a kind of grace.

My mind's eye returned to Abraham. Out of his massive herds of donkeys, he had one special donkey—hand selected for his personal use. Sturdy, sure-footed, and able, this donkey had no idea he was about to become part of one of the most pivotal and prophetic events in biblical history.

I could just see it: One morning, Abraham got up and saddled the donkey for a three-day journey to Mount Moriah. He brought along his young son, Isaac; two servants; and some wood for a sacrifice to worship God. I have no doubt that Abraham lifted Isaac onto his donkey (it was customary for women and children to ride while the men walked) and led him on the long trek.

That first night, they camped under a canopy of brilliant stars, the very stars that had once given the man then called Abram such hope. Abraham squeezed his eyes shut, trying to blot out his memory of God's promise that his descendants would number as countless as the stars. As he lay on his makeshift pallet, he listened to Isaac talking in his sleep and the donkey rustling in the brush. *Only two more days to Moriah,* he thought.

Did Abraham wonder if his God, the one he thought he knew, had changed His mind about His promise? What a torturous night it was. As far as he could see, he had no option but to obey God's command to give up his son.

Perhaps Abraham's donkey walked along willingly in the small caravan of travelers: Abraham, the donkey carrying Isaac, a servant carrying wood, and another servant carrying food . . . all trudging through the wilderness.

But I know donkeys: Like all donkeys, there *had* to have been a few times that he balked.

Refused to go.

Stopped the whole procession.

I can picture the moment: a standoff between man and animal. But rather than take his frustration out on a stubborn donkey, this time Abraham patted the beast of burden on the head. He scratched his ears a little. Abraham, grieving with each step, savored every extra moment he had with Isaac, blissfully chatting away. The father could wait. He could give the donkey a chance to collect his thoughts and decide when to start moving again.

It's what you do when you walk with donkeys: You expect to stop every now and then.

Most days, I imagine Abraham was impatient with his willful donkey.

But these three days . . . oh, how he treasured each stop.

He looked at his boy, his beautiful boy, sitting atop his

daddy's donkey. Perhaps Abraham lamented that Isaac would never see his own donkey—a special donkey Abraham had already picked out for him. This one would have to do . . . a borrowed donkey for a much-loved son, on a journey toward sacrifice. There would be no other donkey.

Abraham's story *would* have ended sadly, except for one thing: *Grace showed up.*

Grace is the unexpected twist to this story, and it's the unexpected twist to *every* story. It's the surprise ending we can hardly dare to hope for.

In the nick of time, God stepped into the awful nightmare and stopped the whole proceeding. God provided a ram—its horns caught in a bush—for the sacrifice. Isaac, the apple of Abraham's eye, was spared and would go on to become a source of blessing for the entire world.

It was a dramatic moment that would be told and retold to Abraham's descendants for thousands of years: *This is our God.*

Our God is full of surprises.

Our God is gracious.

Our God blesses.

Our God will see to it.

Our God will provide.

Yahweh-Yireh.

It was time for a pit stop. Tom exited the freeway and pulled into a Whataburger parking lot. We were hungry and also wanted to check on our tiny passenger to see how he was faring. The sight of fuzzy ears sticking up and the sound of miniature hooves echoing in the trailer grabbed the attention of others, who wandered over for a better look.

One lady stepped onto the bumper of the trailer and peered inside. "Oh, a little donkey!" she exclaimed. Henderson Number Ten's liquid brown eyes gazed at her, his ears perked forward. "Look how cute he is!"

Then she turned to me. "Donkeys always bring me such joy," she said. "You have no idea how much I needed it today." Squeezing my hand, she left without saying anything more.

She didn't have to. I understood.

Just when you think it's the end of your story, grace shows up in all its unexpected glory.

Sometimes, grace arrives as a moment of joy in the middle of despair.

Sometimes, grace's horns get caught in a thicket, at just the right moment.

And sometimes, grace has fuzzy ears, a bristly mane, and hope for a new start.

CHAPTER 2
I Believe

I believe in God, the Father almighty,
creator of heaven and earth.
I believe in Jesus Christ, his only Son, our Lord.
He was conceived by the power of the Holy Spirit
and born of the Virgin Mary.
He suffered under Pontius Pilate,
was crucified, died, and was buried.
He descended to the dead. On the third day he rose again.
He ascended into heaven,
and is seated at the right hand of the Father.
He will come again to judge the living and the dead.
I believe in the Holy Spirit, the holy catholic Church,
the communion of saints, the forgiveness of sins,
the resurrection of the body, and the life everlasting. Amen.

Daily Morning Prayer and Daily Evening Prayer: Rite Two,
"The Apostles' Creed," *The Book of Common Prayer*

The horse trailer, with its one tiny occupant, reverberated like a bass drum as we made our way up the uneven dirt driveway toward the yellow, barn-shaped house at the end. We had named our home "Beulah" when we moved in more than ten years ago. It's a good Southern name more befitting a luxurious mansion at the end of a graceful tree-lined entry than a 1970s fixer-upper that's not even facing the right direction for a proper introduction. A genteel Southern house knows to turn toward guests and present a handsome first impression. Beulah offers a sideways view and a casual over-the-shoulder invitation to enter through the breezeway between the garage and the back sliding-glass door. The door opens into the kitchen, a visitor's second clue that Beulah brushes formality aside. It's hard to be pretentious with a back door that, for all practical purposes, is a front door.

Tom brought the Suburban to a stop, and before getting out to open the pasture gate, I looked over at the house and noticed how Beulah's distinctive eaves resemble a ball cap's bill that's been curved down for maximum shade. A lamp glowed through the living room window. *It's good to be home.*

Now we just needed to safely deposit our new family member into his temporary digs before calling it a day. The little donkey looked bewildered as we coaxed him out of the trailer. I led him slowly into a fenced enclosure inside the pasture. The pen—once housing strange ostrichlike birds when a previous landowner had hoped to cash in on the growing emu-oil craze—would make a suitable place for him to spend his first night. It had a small three-sided shelter made of corrugated tin he could sleep in and a few scraggly trees that would provide some shade in the morning.

"What do you think we should name him?" Tom asked. By now it was after 9 p.m., and there was no sign of Flash nearby. Good. No doubt he was slumbering deep in the woods, unaware of the newcomer.

"It's obvious that Henderson Number Ten should be his official name," I replied. "What if we call him Henry for short? I believe that's what Doc's been calling him, and I think it fits him well. It seems like a good name for a jaunty little fellow."

"Henry." Tom said the name slowly. "I like it."

"The names Flash and Henry go well together, but will the actual donkeys get along?" I wondered aloud, directing Henry to a small pile of hay in the corner of the pen. I pictured them next to each other, Flash reaching his nose down to touch Henry's upturned muzzle.

"Of course they'll get along." Tom seemed confident. "What's there to worry about?"

"Oh, I'm not worried; I'm just excited! I probably won't be able to sleep tonight. I know it's gonna take a few days for them to get used to each other, but right now Flash has no idea that his best friend just arrived." I crouched down and rubbed Henry's ear between my thumb and middle finger. Poor guy— he looked worn out from the long ride. His head slumped and he sighed deeply, too tired to notice much about his new surroundings. Exploration could wait until tomorrow.

I understood completely. By the time I crawled into bed, exhaustion had crept into my bones. I was turning the page to begin another new chapter, one with a lot of unknowns—and it wasn't just about Flash and Henry. As I drifted off, Abraham wandered into my mind once again, now starting his journey home. Isaac was riding his father's faithful donkey. Isaac—the precious son Abraham thought he would have to give up. It was as if his *own* life had been handed back to him. His heart was light and every step a joy.

Yet as much as he was teeming with anticipation and hope for the future, there was more thinking to do. This event in the mountains had shown him that his God was not at all who Abraham thought. He had made assumptions and obeyed the God he thought he knew . . . but then God surprised him in the most incredible way with His last-minute intervention to save Isaac.

Abraham must have sensed that he was starting all over again. Maybe he retraced his own faith journey by going back to square one: *What do I know* for sure *about God? What do I know for certain about my own life? What will be different from this point on?* He had a three-day journey home to begin putting the pieces together—with a donkey at his side.

There was something inspiring about this image that appealed to me. Perhaps walking with a donkey could be a catalyst for figuring out my own life, for wrestling with my own faith and giving me the space and rhythm to ask my own set of questions. The thought of walking with a donkey seemed timeless, as if I would feel the dry desert air surrounding Mount Moriah right here in my pasture in Texas.

An idea began to form in my mind.

Like Abraham, I was on a journey away from the familiar and into uncharted territory.

Before our last child left home, I had felt calm—even a

little elated—as I looked ahead at Life After Kids. I dreamed about how nice it would be to go out to eat more often. How I wouldn't have to plan meals, or go to sports events, or argue about chores and responsibilities. "Just the two of us" sounded wonderfully romantic. Maybe Tom and I would travel more or spend more time on personal creativity. Maybe we'd have people over for fancy dinners or do more with friends. Maybe God would lead us to a new ministry or show us innovative ways to be available to Him. I knew I'd feel sad saying good-bye to motherhood, of course, but I'd somehow manage to grace-fully slide into this new "empty-nest thing" with style.

Boy, was I unprepared.

Tom and I watched Grayson drive down the dirt driveway, slowly maneuvering his freshly washed car to avoid a buildup of dust. The rear-window decal proudly read TEXAS A&M ENGINEERING. As our son embarked into adulthood, his car turning the corner around the big cedar tree and disappearing, my throat seized up.

We, the remaining adults, sat in wooden chairs in the front yard and cried.

I remembered grieving after each of our girls had left. How their shared bedroom had become tidier with each of their departures. Before, I'd fussed at them to pick up their clothes; wanted to know why the lunch bag with a moldy sandwich hadn't been taken out of the backpack; and reminded them numerous times that wet towels needed to be hung up, not left on the bathroom counter. Now I could see the floor for the first time in years, and the beds stayed neatly made, with childhood teddy bears propped on the pillows . . . and I hated it. I mean, I loved that the room was clean, but I hated that it was *empty*.

It was empty of the two beautiful daughters who brought such joy and music and endless conversation to our world. It was empty of all their *life*. For a long time, I couldn't bear to even look in their bedroom, averting my eyes every time I passed by.

At least Grayson was still at home for the next five years. Along with Tom, I helped him navigate his high school years: cheering him on as he played hockey (and pounding on the glass barrier like all good hockey moms do), sitting together on the couch and watching movies, talking late into the night about life. Since I had savored these special times, I finally felt ready to become that chic empty nester I had been dreaming about.

However, "feeling ready" and "being ready" are two different things.

What I didn't plan for was the mental rearranging I needed to do. After being a mom for twenty-six years, I struggled to remember who I was before that first labor. I squinted at my reflection in the mirror. *Is that woman still in there somewhere?* I knew she had been thinner, with no double chin, but beyond that it got a little hazy. *Maybe I need stronger "readers" from Walmart.*

My identity as a believer needed reshaping too. After years of busy church activity, I often felt disconnected from the God who, I suspected, spoke in the quiet I longed for. The quiet had finally arrived, and . . . well, now I wasn't sure what to do with it. I knew how to "do" Christianity, and I did it well. But layers of patterns and doctrines had somehow become "essential" over the years, and unexpectedly, I found myself questioning whether they composed what the Christian life was really supposed to be.

Yet I was afraid to relinquish any of these habits and conventions that had become so comfortable. *Who would I be on the other side of letting go?*

This journey into the unknown was like being pulled out to sea—wondering if I'd be flung back onto the shore I'd started from or end up on a completely different shore altogether.

It was a sensation I knew from experience. As the daughter of missionary parents, I had lived in Mexico for a time during my childhood. When I was twelve and my only sister, Katherine, was ten, we went camping with family friends in Acapulco during spring break. The two of us spent hours playing on the beach and enjoying the water under the relaxed supervision of the adults, oblivious to how scorched we were getting from the tropical sun. (Unfortunately, we didn't know anything about sunscreen then.)

The waves generated by the Pacific Ocean are incredibly powerful in Acapulco, and humans, especially small humans, are no match for riptides. One day, an unusually huge wave crashed over me, immediately followed by another from a different direction.

Suddenly I could no longer touch the sandy bottom, and although I thought I was a good swimmer, without a firm footing I was tossed around like a rag doll in a washing machine. My muscles screamed as I tried to move my arms and kick my legs, vainly attempting to propel myself to shore against the power of the tide that was dragging me out to sea. I choked on the seawater and gulped for air, terrified of being pulled under.

With salt stinging my eyes, I turned just in time to see Katherine's head cresting the farthest wave, with only open ocean beyond—and I knew . . . *She's gone. I'll never see her again.*

I began to panic. Though water pummeled me again and again, I tried to yell for help each time I surfaced. "*Ayuda! Ayúdame!*"

An older man appeared beside me and reached for my hand, pulling me in to safety. *Oh, thank You, God!*

"My sister, *mi hermana!*" I sobbed and choked as I stumbled on the sand, trying to find my balance on shaky legs. Shielding my eyes from the sun with my hands, I frantically scanned the ocean for Katherine. *There!* Her head was still bobbing.

Just then I saw another man wading out toward her, waist deep in the water. Was he an angel? I didn't know, but that ocean *should* have been over his head. The next thing I knew, Katherine was in his arms, and he was making his way through the waves toward me and the man who had rescued me. Water dripped from Katherine's hero as he gently placed her next to me on the sand. "*Estás bien?* Are you okay?"

My sister and I nodded as we huddled next to each other. Wrapped in towels, we sat on the beach with our chins on our knees, holding hands tightly, knowing we'd been at death's doorstep and miraculously survived.

The pull of the water, the sand being sucked out from beneath your feet, the utter powerlessness in the grip of such a natural force, the fear of going under and drowning . . . it's something you never forget.

I was experiencing that same force now, except this time the pull was toward something I couldn't explain. I was afraid, yes; and yet I sensed this mystery could be deep and beautiful and mysterious. This "something" (or Someone) was asking me to let go of my tightly held ideas and patterns, and, like Abraham, to simply trust.

Flash lumbered sleepily out of the woods as the birds chirped their cheery morning choruses. In typical fashion, his head was knee high, eyes so fixed on the path in front of him that he was startled to find Tom and me standing in his way, as if we'd materialized out of thin air. He's a lot like me before I've had my first cup of coffee, just plod, plod, plodding to the kitchen with a single, groggy focus. *Don't talk to me. Better yet, don't even look at me.*

"Flash, come meet your new friend!" I spoke softly as I wiped the sleep from his eyes with my sleeve.

He looked at me in utter disbelief, offended that I would ask him to do anything first thing in the morning. Yawning, he refused to comply with my request for several minutes. It was like he was hitting the snooze button one last time. Eventually he managed to follow me to the pen, where Tom was waiting for us.

Henry stood inside, facing us at attention with his head up, ears forward, and eyes wide. He had seen Flash coming and shivered with excitement, his shiny dark coat glistening in the early sunlight. Flash stopped in his tracks. He shook his head to chase the cobwebs out of his consciousness, then flared his nostrils at the scent of this obvious intruder.

Approaching with caution, he put his ears back and inched his nose closer to the chain-link fence. Henry's ears were still pricked as he stepped closer, bringing his own nose to the fence. Nose to nose, they introduced themselves to each other while Tom and I held our collective breath. Flash's ears swiveled back into their normal position, and the two looked at each other, mesmerized.

"This is going great," I whispered to Tom, pleased with our initial success. We fist-bumped in silent victory.

The moment was short-lived. Just then, Flash stomped his

front feet and blew loudly through his nose, startling Henry (and us) into jumping back. Henry spun in a circle, then lurched forward with a squeal, rattling the fence with force. At that, Flash took off running down the length of the pen, with Henry in hot pursuit on the inside. They froze simultaneously at the far end and stared each other down, this time with both sets of ears laid flat.

And then . . . Henry exploded. Doc was not kidding. With jet-propelled "fuel" (er, waste) spraying from his backside, he rocketed toward us—bucking, braying, and dashing as fast as his little legs could carry him. Flash followed suit, moving quickly with his head low to the ground and grunting madly. Back and forth they went, coming to a standstill every few minutes to sniff each other through the fence. Flash was locked on every movement Henry made.

Then it hit me: *Flash has never seen another donkey!* He had no clue what to make of this long-eared animal who had landed in his pasture without an invitation—*What in the world was this animal?*

I pondered further. *Wait! If Flash doesn't know what a donkey is, that means he doesn't even know he is a donkey!*

For a while, Flash was good friends with some cows who had lived in an adjacent field. They adored him, making him one of their own. He enjoyed every opportunity to hang out at the fence with the bovines. Later, horses showed up in a neighboring pasture, and they seemed to accept Flash as one of the herd, even though (in my opinion) they acted superior whenever they could. The stallions would prance by him with a head toss and tail flip, and Flash would respond with a head toss and tail flip of his own. He wasn't nearly as graceful, but he certainly tried.

Then, of course, there was the unexpected friend he'd made, but . . . well, I couldn't bear to think about her now.

I'm sure Flash was convinced that he was either a really smart cow or a short, spirited horse. Why would he think otherwise?

Now, along came Henry—Flash's Mini-Me, a dude with long ears and markings that looked strangely familiar. Suddenly, Flash had some mental rearranging to do. Call me a genius, but I could see this would take a little more time than I had originally thought.

I looked at my watch. We had other things to do that day besides waiting for friendship to blossom, so we reluctantly left Henry inside the pen for the rest of the day. At least the fence between them offered some degree of safety as they finished sizing each other up.

When we returned in the evening, it appeared the donkeys had worn themselves out. Their level of intensity had been reduced to "calmly interested"—much better for opening the gate. I quietly slipped into the pen so I could begin to bond with Henry before letting him out. Henry saw me enter and turned his entire body away from me, but at least he stood still.

"Okay, we can start with back here," I said softly. I scratched above his tail, then slowly worked my fingers up to his head. Under Flash's watchful gaze, I massaged Henry's ears, my heart melting when he closed his eyes in delight. Maybe no one had ever taken the time to rub them. Poor baby.

Finally, it was time. I stood with my hand on the chain, ready to unlock it . . . and then hesitated. I knew everything was going to change—for both Henry and Flash—the moment the gate opened.

This is how it is, isn't it?

Just when you get comfortable with where you are, somebody opens a gate and introduces a whole new set of variables. Behind the security of a fence, it's all good. You can *see* what's on the other side; you feel confident in your ability to interact with it . . . and then reality collides with fantasy. You realize that what you thought you knew is woefully inadequate for this new paradigm.

"I think you can do this now," I said to Henry as I pushed the gate open. He looked up at me like he understood what I was saying. His mane stood at attention, and his wispy tail signaled his eagerness. I looked at Flash, whose head was down and ears were back. "Unfortunately, I don't know if you'll ever be ready, buddy."

Tom was capturing the proceedings on video and stepped aside to let Henry pass. Henry rushed directly over to Flash, ears forward and nostrils wide, as if to say, "Hello, new friend!"

Flash stood motionless, his head still low as Henry approached. His skin quivered. Their noses touched.

I held my breath.

For a moment, one small moment, it was perfect.

Suddenly, Flash blew through his nose and stomped his feet. Henry was taken by surprise and jumped back. Flash stomped again, shaking his head and making a run at Henry, who backed up even farther.

Henry made a few more attempts to get close, but each time, Flash chased him off. When Henry tried one last time, Flash simply laid his ears back and turned away. His body language was plain: "I'm not interested."

Bewildered, Henry also wheeled around, the two of them

facing opposite directions. The small donkey glanced over his shoulder at the bigger donkey, who shot him a look of mistrust, then grunted and walked away.

Henry apparently didn't get the message. He followed Flash, stopping near him but turning to face away once again.

Flash wheezed and stamped his front hooves to scare the interloper.

Startled, Henry bucked, hitting Flash squarely in the chest with his back feet. Flash responded with his own kick, which missed Henry by a mile. Henry spun around and nipped at Flash, who bolted into the open field, clearly confused. A moment later, Henry headed in his direction.

I winced. *Oh dear. How will Flash ever realize he's a donkey if he refuses to even engage with one?* I looked from one to the other: a shaggy brownish-gray donkey (who now appeared huge by comparison) and a new little chocolate-colored guy, both with their back ends toward each other. It was a woeful start.

"We're just going to have to give them time. Eventually they'll get along . . . they have no choice!" Tom's voice of reason tamped down my worries.

Just then, Henry's rotund frame began to heave—a bray was about to erupt. He squeezed his eyes shut and let loose.

"Hee . . . hee . . . hee . . . HAW! HEE-haw, HEE-haw!"

It was the squeakiest excuse for a bray I'd ever heard. Simply laughable! It broke through the drama with comic relief and got Flash's attention. Flash whipped around so fast I was afraid he might hurt himself. Ears forward, body trembling, nostrils flaring.

Hey, that's just like the sound I *make!* I imagined him saying. He pawed at the ground and shook his ears.

Henry's pitiful bray subsided with a last, prolonged *"haaaw,"* after which he opened his eyes and looked around. His gaze came to rest on Flash, and he tilted his head in question. If he'd had eyebrows, they would have been raised.

Flash remained where he was and nodded. *Wow! You speak my language.*

It was a small step in the right direction.

The road to friendship was going to be rocky. Until this moment, Flash had lived his entire life not really knowing who—or what—he really was. He was going to need to peel away the cow and horse identities he'd assumed. It took seeing "the real thing" to help him discover the donkeyness that was always inside him.

I guess I was looking for my own "donkeyness," longing for a simple, uncomplicated life and faith at my core. I had a sense that where my faith was concerned, I'd need to start at square one. Maybe it sounds crazy for someone who has been a Christian pretty much her entire life to really begin asking questions—the most basic ones—for the first time.

Who is Jesus?

What does it mean to be a Christian?

What did Jesus say about Himself?

Which doctrines are essential to the gospel and which are nonessential?

What can I let go of while still being faithful to Christ?

Is it okay to be asking these questions now in my fifties?

I just wanted . . . I just wanted my faith to have integrity. I wanted to strip away anything superfluous so I could know if what I had was real.

∧ ∧

That fall, I decided the only way forward was to go back to the beginning and embrace the journey. I dipped my toes into church history, spent time in the Gospels, and hung on the words of Jesus, who astounded me with His presence and message. I found a historical feast that spanned the centuries and encompassed the flavors of cultures and times. I began to get acquainted with the early church's fathers and mothers, the fiery preachers of the Reformation and the Great Awakening, as well as thinkers and writers of the present day.

The world outside my gate was wide, colorful, and full of life. It was multilayered and textured—as dizzyingly diverse as the numerous bird species on earth. When I learned there were thousands of Christian denominations, of which I belonged to *just one*, I was taken aback. My modern American Evangelicalism was only a tiny fraction of the wider church. Yet somehow I'd been under the impression that the way "we" do it is the only "right" way.

Surely there *had* to be a common core of beliefs everyone agreed upon. Beneath the layers, I wanted to find the spiritual DNA strand linking all the species to one family.

I didn't have to look far: I found it in Jesus Himself. As I spent time in the Gospel narratives, I began to see Him as I never had before. I loved the way He welcomed outcasts, women, sinners, children—those on the fringes of society. I saw how He answered questions by posing His own in return, turning people's ideas about the God they thought they knew on their heads. He was tough on those who wielded power but gentle with those who had none. He had no qualms about ruffling the feathers of religious people but soothed the weary around Him with a message of hope and forgiveness. Jesus' teachings were sometimes hard to understand and even more difficult to put into practice; yet they were always compelling. His invitation— "Follow Me!"—went straight to my heart, and I knew He was Someone truly worthy of being followed. No wonder His disciples risked everything to be known as people of "the Way."

Jesus' first followers would offer more clues. *How did they see the gospel of Christ? What did they believe about Him? How did they tell people about their newfound faith?*

I struck gold in the Nicene Creed and the Apostles' Creed. Hammered out in AD 325 at the Council of Nicaea in what is Turkey today, the Nicene Creed brought together a structure of orthodox beliefs for an increasingly disparate church. It expanded on the Apostles' Creed, which had been in existence (at least orally) since first-century Christians began to share their faith.

The simplicity and clarity of their ancient words stunned me as I realized how beautifully they represent Christianity's DNA—the original beliefs that connect us and make us brothers and sisters in Christ.

I guess the Creeds fell out of favor as an unnecessary recitation in corporate worship, I mused. Personally, I had rarely even heard them referenced in my nondenominational circles. I had never been encouraged to affirm the Creeds in my personal devotions. I never once considered teaching them to my children, who had also not learned them in Sunday school. They simply had never been a part of my life, even though I'd spent that lifetime as a Christian.

Finding the Apostles' Creed was more exciting than getting

DNA results back from Ancestry.com! I could now trace my spiritual heritage all the way back to the first century, to a time closely connected with Jesus' earthly life and ministry. If I closed my eyes, I could imagine being a woman then, a new believer without easy access to the Scriptures, but whose recitations of the Creed were as vital as the water she regularly went to retrieve. Perhaps she walked to the well beside a donkey, the precious words of her faith echoing in her heart as she loaded the heavy containers onto her beast of burden.

I brought out my small red notebook and carefully wrote the Apostles' Creed inside. It fit into my pocket, a perfect reference to carry with me as I did my own modern-day chores of filling the donkeys' water buckets and mucking out the barn.

I believe in God, the Father almighty . . .

I believe.

Simple, uncluttered. The words of the Apostles' Creed are the "good bones" that provide the framework for all our other doctrines and preferences. I was coming to see how as Christians we may differ on certain matters like end-time theology, baptism, predestination, worship styles and traditions, and gifts of the Spirit—among a whole host of other matters. So often I'd let myself get caught up in making these the criteria for whom I would fellowship with, making judgment calls on who was "in" or "out." I made the mistake of thinking my identity was found in these nonessentials, and I focused on matters that divide rather than unite us.

God's family is bigger than I imagined or gave Him credit for. At our core, we Christians—Orthodox, Charismatic,

Presbyterian, Catholic, Evangelical, Reformed, and others—
share the same genetic code that makes us family.

∧ ∧

The crisp air and the colorful leaves that remained on the trees
beckoned me outside one afternoon. Henry had been with us
for a while and seemed to be settling in, and I wanted to spend
some quality time with Flash to assure him that he was still
the star of my show. I thought a short walk around the pasture
together would be a good way to connect. I brought Flash's halter out of the tack room and put it on him while Henry looked
on with interest from a distance.

With a sideways glance at Henry, Flash took one step forward and then stopped. He refused to budge. I tried every trick
in the book to get him to follow my lead: gentle pressure, verbal
commands, carrot bribes . . . but he was too distracted by his
new pasture mate to pay any attention to what I was asking
him to do.

Perhaps Flash was fixing Henry in his mind. Maybe he
needed time to let new information sink in, and he had to
rearrange his thoughts. Maybe he felt himself being pulled by
waves into a new paradigm and couldn't be rushed.

I believe he was discovering his identity, the very soul of
who he was.

I believe I was too.

Yes, I do believe.

CHAPTER 3

All That I Need

The LORD is my shepherd; I have all that I need.
He lets me rest in green meadows;
he leads me beside peaceful streams.
He renews my strength.
He guides me along right paths,
bringing honor to his name.
Even when I walk
through the darkest valley,
I will not be afraid,
for you are close beside me.
Your rod and your staff
protect and comfort me.
You prepare a feast for me
in the presence of my enemies.
You honor me by anointing my head with oil.
My cup overflows with blessings.
Surely your goodness and unfailing love will pursue me
all the days of my life,
and I will live in the house of the LORD forever.

Psalm 23

My dreams of Flash and Henry becoming instant best buds crashed and burned almost immediately. *These things take time,* I reminded myself. Besides, not all friends hit it off from the start, so why should I expect these donkeys to love each other like brothers from day one? If human friendships require time and effort, it would stand to reason that animals would need the same.

I reviewed the facts: Both donkeys were seven or eight years old and considered adults. Both had been gelded recently, and our vet forewarned us they could remain "more aggressive" until their raging hormone levels settled down. We didn't know much about Henry's past, other than that he was found wandering around with a large drove of donkeys. Flash, on the other hand, had been an "only child" in our pasture for years.

Their new normal would take some getting used to.

Doc Darlin had also given us a heads-up about miniature donkeys. "Lotta times, these little guys have some kind of complex. They want to make up for their short height by beating up on the big guys. I don't know about this one here, but don't be surprised if he tries to be the boss."

A word to the wise.

Turned out, Henry was the most delightful little donkey in the world—so shy he couldn't approach me without first turning around and backing in, just to be on the safe side. He was willing to let me brush him for several minutes at a time, and he allowed me to lead him with a halter for short distances before deciding it was enough. Henry's gentle disposition was endearing.

At least, that's how he was with *me*.

With Flash, it was another story.

When they weren't ignoring each other, they bickered over everything.

Hey, I was here first.

No, I *want to graze here.*

No, I *do!*

You're bugging me.

No, you're *bugging* me.

Henry followed Flash around like a pesky little brother, invading his space. Flash tried to get away whenever he could, but Henry was persistent. He continued to needle Flash, biting and nipping at his legs and neck. One day I watched out the window in horror as Henry chomped down on Flash's neck and wheeled him around. Dust flew all around as Flash struggled to stay on his feet. Flash let out a high-pitched wheeze and tried to pull back. I could see his alarm as he was brought down to his knees and Henry kicked at him.

I threw open the door and ran to the fence, yelling and clapping my hands to break it up. Only then did Henry let go. He sprang to meet me with a last buck in Flash's direction, then acted as if he were completely innocent, shaking his ears and cocking his head as charmingly as possible.

I was too angry to speak to him. I looked past Henry to Flash—my beautiful Flash, whom nobody had better mess with. He appeared dazed.

"Flash, oh Flashy! Are you okay?" I reached for the bigger

donkey's face as he approached, then inspected the bite wounds on his neck. He was bleeding.

Henry stood off to the side and bent forward, scratching his front leg with his teeth like nothing had happened—which only made me more upset.

"Henderson Number Ten, you cannot do this. You've got to stop!" I forcefully lectured him while he simply blinked back at me with his soulful brown eyes.

It's hard to stay mad at someone that cute, but a glance back at poor Flash made it possible.

∧ ∧

Over the next few days, I found myself constantly looking out the window to make sure Henry wasn't killing Flash. Fresh wounds appeared regularly on Flash's neck, and I became worried that the mayhem would never end.

I messaged Doc, sending a photo of one particularly egregious bite mark. "Is this normal?" I asked. I was ready to send Henry packing if he kept it up.

"Yep, that looks pretty awful," he replied, "but don't worry. This is typical behavior while they figure things out. Looks like Flash is going to have to get tough with Henry."

The last thing I needed was for things to escalate. I wanted them to figure it out *now*. This wasn't at all what I'd imagined companionship to look like.

As disappointed as I felt, I decided I would wait a while longer before asking to borrow the big horse trailer again. I kept the phone number handy, though, just in case.

Both donkeys had put on weight over the winter months. The plentiful winter ryegrass, which voluntarily grows in the pasture in cooler temperatures, presented them with a daily feast they took full advantage of. Flash, with his extra pounds, simply looked bigger and stronger—his appearance enhanced by a bushy cold-weather coat. Henry . . . well, Henry just looked like a chubster. His belly resembled a water balloon, stretching out from his narrow backbone into a portly shape, balanced precariously on four short legs. His thick winter hair gave him a teddy bear appearance, which definitely helped me let go of my grudge. Despite my impatience to reach my goals for their relationship, I tried to remain hopeful.

I watched for any "off" behavior that might be a symptom of illness, and of course with all that grass, I kept an eye on their weight, looking for fatty rolls developing on their necks and backs—an indication of obesity. In the past, Flash's extra heft had come off as soon as summer hit, and it soon proved true for Henry, too. Their winter coats were also starting to come off. I was surprised that Henry shed his first; he looked downright sleek for weeks before Flash lost his shaggy hair. Flash had a decidedly patchy between-season look that was especially shabby next to Henry's gleaming summer do.

^ ^

In early summer, the pasture still seemed green from a distance. The tall weeds and vegetation might have fooled someone into thinking there was plenty to eat out there, at least at a glance. It was only up close that you could see the dry ground was bereft of anything nutritious. Still, it was beautiful under the blue Texas sky. The prickly pear cactus plants (*nopales* in Spanish) showed off their yellow and pink blooms, shaped like floppy beach hats upturned in the sun. The pungent aroma of sage filled the air as the donkeys brushed the shrubs' leaves, releasing a minty perfume. By now the tall grasses had seeded out, and their dry stalks made a slight *shhh* in the breeze, as if insisting upon quiet contemplation in the field.

The LORD is my shepherd . . .

Did I mention *chiggers*? Anyone from the South will probably just shudder simply reading the word. You know what I'm talking about. A short walk through the pasture smells wonderful, but you pay the price with a dozen chigger bites from ankles to waist. The nearly microscopic juvenile mites clump together in the tall grass and jump on passersby faster than you can say "ouch!" Chiggers embed themselves under your skin and itch like crazy for up to two weeks at a time— worse than mosquito bites.

One night, Tom happened upon me while I was applying clear nail polish to the red welts along my waistline.

"You know that doesn't work, don't you?"

"Well, they burrowed into my skin, and I'm trying to suffocate them," I said, twisting to reach the bite on my back.

"Old wives' tale," he said.

Well, I am one of the old, er, mature wives.

The next morning, I awoke to the sound of the riding lawn mower. Tom knew how much my walks in the pasture meant to me, so he proceeded to extend the existing path he'd made earlier in the year to include the entire perimeter of the fields, along with some gently curving connecting paths. I saw that he followed many of Flash's well-worn trails, widening them from single lanes to double. *Thank you.*

He also knew the shorter grass would lessen the chigger attacks and, most of all, make it easier for me to enjoy my time outside. What a gift. What made it even more meaningful was that this path was becoming so much more than a means of exercise or alone time for me and the donkeys.

It was becoming my prayer path.

My little red notebook, where I had first jotted down "The General Thanksgiving" just before we picked up Henry, now contained several handwritten prayers, psalms, and the Apostles' Creed to refer to as I walked.

I was implementing the "KonMari" method of spiritual housecleaning: Clear everything out; then examine each belief or practice. Either thank the item for its service and let it go, or carefully invite selected things back in, one at a time, finding treasured spots for the customs and tenets that bring you joy. Such was the only way I could think of to declutter and rearrange.

On this particular day, I decided to meditate on the Twenty-third Psalm. This one was a keeper forever; I could never let go of it. The combination of pasture and poetry put my soul in a contemplative, joyful mood.

> *The LORD is my shepherd;*
> *I have all that I need . . .*

As I prayed, the path took me around a clump of cedar trees toward the back pasture.

God, You are my Guide and my Provider. There is no lack in You. I have nothing to fear because You are with me.

My sudden emergence through the trees surprised Flash and Henry, who were surrounded by a thick cloud of dust in the middle of the brush. They froze midbite, knowing they'd just been caught fighting. Instantly, they pretended they'd just been horsing around, but I wasn't fooled.

The brown haze they'd kicked up swirled around their feet and drifted off into the trees, reminding me that the grass they loved to graze had disappeared with the change of season. Flash trotted over, with Henry following behind at a distance, looking for a handout. I knew it was time to start supplementing their diet with hay. I made a mental note to make a stop at Texas A+ Feed.

Back in its heyday, Texas A+ Feed stocked every kind of farm supply you might need. It devoted a large area to upscale saddles and tack and took pride in its selection of fancy cowboy boots and colorful Western wear. When we'd first started shopping there—to purchase dog food in bulk long before we had donkeys—I was wowed by the merchandise. Now, the shelves stood nearly empty.

Once considered out in the country, the store was now surrounded by urban sprawl. It wasn't in close proximity to its former customer base of farmers and ranchers, who had moved farther out into the country, so business had dwindled. The last time I was inside, I had spotted dusty spray bottles of fly repellent, soap, an assortment of tack, and odds and ends such as kitchenware, watches, and belts, all heaped on a folding table. A handwritten neon-pink SALE sign was taped to one edge.

As I did on each visit, I maneuvered around the used cars, boats, and junk behind the building to get to the loading dock.

Every time I stepped out of the Suburban here, I vowed to stop coming, to find a closer supplier.

Bill, an older African American man in charge of the warehouse, wheeled the forklift to a stop when he saw me. "Well, hey there, little lady!" he said in his booming voice. "What are we getting today?" He smiled.

"Four bales of coastal."

"I'll go get some good ones for you. These are too old." He backed away from the stack at the end of the dock and disappeared.

Bill was the only reason I kept coming back to Texas A+ Feed and Auto, as the sign now said. I appreciated his cheery disposition, especially since learning through our conversations that he'd been battling cancer, and it was getting difficult for him to hoist hay bales and feed bags.

Most bales are composed of either grass or legumes that are compressed and readily separated into about sixteen sections called flakes, making it easier to grab the amount you need at feeding time. Since the donkeys browsed in the pasture all day, they really wouldn't need much hay to stay healthy. One flake for each donkey, morning and night, would be sufficient in the summer months. At this rate, we'd burn through almost two bales a week, and in a couple of weeks I'd go back to the store, vow to never return, see Bill, and then decide to give Texas A+ Feed and Auto one more chance. I would repeat this exercise for the rest of the summer.

As I was driving up to the barn, I could see Flash and Henry watching me closely before hustling over to investigate. I backed the Suburban up to where Tom was waiting, parked, and went around to the back. I opened the hatch, the intoxicating aroma of fresh hay greeting me while, out of the corner of my eye, I saw Henry push Flash out of the way so he would have the best view.

Flash certainly loves feeding time. They must both be hungry.

My first mistake was putting the hay into one single pile for both to eat from. Yeah, not cool.

Henry wanted all of it.

All. Of. It.

He would not let Flash even get close.

He bucked and kicked his striped little legs at Flash, then raced back and forth between Flash and the hay to keep him away.

Ears back and head down, Flash tried going around him to the left.

Henry bucked him back.

Flash tried sneaking past on the right.

Henry put his head down and charged.

Back and forth the little guy dashed, snorting and kicking. His rotund middle, with its light underbelly, swayed with each movement. I stifled a laugh.

"Okay, Henry. I know how we can fix this."

I scooped up half the hay and created a separate pile several feet away. Now they could both belly up to the bar and enjoy their portions.

Nope.

Henry wanted his pile, *and* he wanted Flash's pile.

He began running interference on Flash, his portly body surprisingly nimble.

Flash laid his ears back flat and tried to get at one of the piles, but he was rebuffed again. As dirt flew in all directions, he grunted his displeasure at the determined little donkey.

I stood back and watched the fray over the hay. Henry was so intent on keeping Flash away that he couldn't enjoy a single tasty bite himself.

Oh Henry.

It was a classic move by someone who had known scarcity.

When you're not sure when—or if—you'll get to eat again, you hoard what you have to avert the possibility of going without.

"Henry, Henry!" I tried to get his attention. "There's plenty for both of you!"

Henry's fixation affected his hearing. There was no talking sense to him.

I set out more hay—more than they could eat in one feeding.

Finally, Henry's hunger won out. He chose the biggest mound and began to eat, pawing at the flake to loosen it. Turning his backside toward Flash to defensively guard his portion, he kept his ears tilted backward so he could sense exactly where Flash was every second.

Flash hung back, then tentatively approached the far side of his pile, eyeing Henry, ears up and alert. Somehow, I think he figured out that Henry still had lingering emotional issues— a few tender spots left inside that hadn't healed yet. Flash let Henry settle in and begin eating before he started to nibble.

Henry had (and still has) a scarcity mind-set.

He was afraid there wouldn't be enough.

He was afraid that if he didn't fight for his share, he wouldn't get any at all.

He was afraid that if he let Flash get the hay, then he might go hungry.

Henry would rather have done without by running himself ragged than risk Flash eating any of *his* portion.

He was so busy keeping Flash at bay that he couldn't enjoy the bounty.

Poor Henry.

A scarcity mind-set had prevented him from experiencing the abundance all around him.

And it wasn't just the hay he felt protective of, but carrots and attention, too.

Sweet and docile Henry became cantankerous and territorial when his worst fears come out—fears born from deprivation, from lacking what he needed. Scarcity locked him into a constant state of anxiousness—comparing who got what, how much, and when. He was certain he was the victim, always getting the short end of the stick.

I couldn't be upset with him. He didn't know why he was frantically reacting this way. In fact, his expression seemed to imply, *Somebody help me! I want to stop kicking, but I just can't!*

Watching Henry, I realized how easy it was for me to let the wounds of the past dictate my actions, even without realizing it. I leaned back on a barn post and recalled how in the early 2000s, Tom and I had followed our dreams to create an art and mural business in the Dallas area. For many years life was exciting—we had more projects than we could handle, and we loved using our talents in a big way by creating beautiful spaces for people. I felt successful and fulfilled.

Then came the housing crisis, when projects became more difficult to find and there was less money for the ones we *could* find. Finally came that fateful day in September 2008, right at the brink of the banking and housing collapse. I vividly remember Tom and I working in the beautiful home of a banking executive, both of us listening to the news on our headsets. *Would his bank be next?* I could barely breathe, let alone hold a paintbrush steady to create a beautiful scene.

"Please, God, let us finish this project, and let us get paid and get out of here before this bank goes under!" we urgently prayed, working even harder to wrap things up. The stress and tangible fear of that moment in time is seared into my consciousness. Millions of people would be impacted by the crisis, but we could only think about our own situation. We needed this paycheck because we didn't have any other projects scheduled. From that day on, it was as if a faucet had been wrenched shut—literally overnight no one was spending any money on luxury items. Least of all on murals and art.

Our client's bank did fail, but not before the check cleared.

Tom and I breathed a sigh of relief, but the sense of our own personal failure had left its mark.

How could God have allowed us to follow our dreams, only to hang us out to dry? We'd poured our souls into doing something that made the best of our talents, that glorified Him, that provided for our family . . . and now our dream (and livelihood) was crushed. Maybe my ideas about God's role in our lives were completely wrong.

It would take years to retool and recover. Meanwhile, our kids were launching into college and marriage, and there were other bills to be paid as well. Starting over at our age seemed impossible.

I understand your scarcity mind-set, little donkey.

Even when endless goodness and bountiful provision are in

plain sight, you worry that you won't have enough, that you *aren't* enough, that you'll never *be* enough. You become possessive and afraid. You hide your true self from others in an effort to preserve what little piece of yourself you are convinced is left. At least that's what I did.

Henry's actions didn't have anything to do with the present moment. They had everything to do with the wounds of his past. Flash wasn't trying to take any of his hay—he wasn't even bothering him. Henry's survival instincts made him lash out, and Flash's natural response seemed to confirm Henry's anxieties. Flash kicked at Henry and tried to shove him out of the way.

"See?" Henry accused. "Flash really *is* trying to steal my food."

Henry's fears had become self-fulfilling. I knew all about that: I recalled how early in my art career, I was guilty of assuming someone might reject me because I didn't have a college degree. Then I'd feel the need to point out my expertise to impress that person. Not surprisingly, I was often rejected—not because I lacked credentials but because I was trying too hard to prove myself. Yet to me, the rejection confirmed what I believed deep inside: I really wasn't good enough.

Now as I began to question some of my belief practices and wanted to reconstruct them in new ways, I retreated from people I held dear. I didn't want to lose their respect, and I feared rejection if I were to bare my doubts and expose my insecurities after a lifetime of being so certain about everything.

"How are you doing? What's going on with you?" My neighbor Priscilla had stopped in to say hello, see Flash, and meet

Henry. We'd been close friends for more than a decade—since the day she hired me to paint her first baby's nursery. We loved watching each other's families grow up and treasured the kind of relationship that could pick up at any time, even when busy schedules kept us from visiting regularly.

Priscilla was happy Flash had a new friend to keep him company. She'd known him since he arrived on our doorstep and loved the fact that her boys enjoyed coming over to feed him carrots. Tom and I were going out of town for a week, and Priscilla's youngest son had volunteered to look after the donkeys for us. Priscilla wanted to make sure she knew what needed to be done in case he needed help.

"Doing great! Never better!" I heard myself say. My heart was too tender to share, my thoughts too unformed. How could I tell her I had gone back to square one in my faith? That I still believed in God but was clinging to Jesus, the Apostles' Creed, some old prayers, and a few psalms to keep me afloat? Everything else was on the table, and I was scared.

Priscilla is a powerhouse of faith and biblical wisdom, and also one of the most genuine and kind people on the face of this earth. We stood by the fence scratching the donkeys and catching up on each other's lives. I knew I could confide in her, and yet . . .

"Are you sure?" she queried, looking into my eyes for clues. *Here was my chance!*

"Oh, you know, I've got my usual stressors . . . work, and kids, and donkeys," I joked, hoping to change the subject.

In that moment, I reasoned I'd be judged by Priscilla in the same way I'd been judged by others in the past. Instead of remembering that our friendship was itself a source of tremendous grace, I just couldn't bring myself to be that vulnerable.

I know, God. I still have a long way to go. Maybe after I get things figured out, then I'll share.

Deep inside, I wanted to tell her that I was struggling, but I had done such a good job of making light of things that the conversation shifted. When I saw how easily she transitioned, I told myself, *Maybe she doesn't really want to know.* I had missed my opportunity to be honest.

I knew I wasn't being fair to our friendship by putting up such walls, but I couldn't help myself. I needed time.

^ ^

As the weeks passed, I continued to watch Henry's frenetic antics, and my heart swelled with compassion for this small donkey. He had been scarred by lack of food and was also starved for attention. No one had ever loved him. It had taken courage for him to trust us and begin to feel at home in these new surroundings. He was doing his best to befriend Flash in the only way he knew how. Rather than judge Henry, I wanted to help him overcome his wounds, to assure him there would always be enough of everything he needed. Hey, I was willing to frequent Texas A+ Feed and Auto every other week for his hay. I wanted him to realize he could always trust me.

I was beginning to put two and two together. *How much more does my heavenly Father look compassionately at me?* At us? How much more does He want you and me to trust Him wholly? The psalmist distills it beautifully, apropos in this pastoral setting:

The LORD is my shepherd; I have all that I need.

There is no lack. We shall not want for anything.

In our woundedness, in our fear of not being enough, or perhaps in our fear that *God* is not enough, we hide our true selves from others and from Him. My journey of rediscovering God and His purposes in the world wasn't an easy path, but I was determined. In the midst of my struggles to make sense of things, I felt bedrock forming beneath my feet: God's purpose is to restore *all things* in creation, including all that we lack within ourselves. He forgives our sins and tends to our wounds, soothing the places that are tender to the touch.

After Jesus recounted the parable of the Good Shepherd to a gathered crowd, he assured them, "I came that [you] may have life, and have it abundantly" (John 10:10, NASB). He promised His life would course through our entire being, but we will experience that abundance *only* when we give ourselves completely to Him.

I sensed God whisper, *See? You can trust Me.*

Each summer when the donkeys' diet calls for supplemental hay, it takes a week of consistently setting out more than they can possibly eat before Henry figures out *there will always be enough.*

After several days of receiving generous portions, he can actually relax. He takes a nap and lets his guard down. He knows he can leave leftover mounds of hay for Flash to eat if he'd like. And when he's hungry, he comes back to snack. He can enjoy his pile of hay without hoarding it.

Henry is learning that there is enough.

It's simple, really.

God always supplies all that we need.

From this place of abundance, I finally felt ready to process everything that had happened before Henry arrived.

I was ready to think about Penny.

CHAPTER 4
Open Our Eyes

O heavenly Father,
who hast filled the world with beauty:
Open our eyes to behold
thy gracious hand in all thy works;
that, rejoicing in thy whole creation,
we may learn to serve
thee with gladness;
for the sake of him through whom
all things were made,
thy Son Jesus Christ our Lord. Amen.

Prayers for the World: "For Joy in God's Creation,"
The Book of Common Prayer

"What is *that*?" Tom looked up from his desk in our home office where he was eating his lunch. It was a late spring day, two years before we had adopted Henry, when Flash was still alone. Tom dropped his sandwich and ran to the window for a better look while I crowded in behind him. A furry brown animal had bolted across the backyard and skidded to a stop at Flash's fence. *Was it a bear?*

When the intruder stopped moving and reared up, then pawed at the ground and tossed its head, we recognized it as a small, shaggy pony. Tom and I gave each other a "just when you think no more stray animals will arrive" look as we ran to the door.

Before we could even get outside, the copper-brown pony was off again, this time galloping down the driveway along the tree-lined fence. Just then, from inside the pasture, Flash barreled toward us, nostrils flaring and sucking in air for a giant bellow. He hit the brakes in a clatter of hooves, his head jutted forward, lips pulled back. *"HEE-HAW, HEE-HAW, HEE-HAW!"* The sound was enormous.

Flash wheeled in a circle, agitated and excited and looking in all directions. Then with a jerky leap, he bolted along the fence in the direction of the brown pony, dirt clods flinging in his wake. Within seconds he was thundering back, the pony accompanying him on the opposite side of the fence and her long, dark tail flying behind her. They met up at the gate.

And that's when we knew what was up.

It was obviously love at first sight. Or sniff, perhaps.

And, clearly, a dangerous situation. The ferocity with which the two tried to reach one another forced us to step back and strategize.

Squealing in delight, the pony took off down the driveway, mirrored step for step by our infatuated donkey, who was moving faster than I'd ever seen him go.

"I'll grab a rope, you get some sweet feed, and we'll try to catch the pony," Tom shouted, knowing any attempt would likely be futile in the face of such physical obsession. With the two of them now at the far end of the pasture, we let ourselves in and sprinted to the barn for our supplies.

Suddenly, there was a huge crash and the sound of splintering wood.

"You don't think . . . ," I whispered.

"Good grief. Flash broke the fence," Tom said, grimacing. It wasn't the first time Flash had broken some fences in the name of love. Tom hoisted the rope over his shoulder and put his game face on for what was now a recovery mission involving not one, but *two* loose equines under the influence of Mother Nature. Although they were somewhat contained by a boundary fence along the edge of our property and the adjoining land belonging to our neighbors Bridgette and Steve, it still meant a good twenty-five acres to cover.

Where the mare had come from was a mystery. We thought we knew about most of the nearby farms and properties with horses, but we had never seen her before. Now we stood helplessly by with our rope and rubber feed dish. Even if we could have gotten close enough for Tom to attach a rope, it would have been dangerous to try to separate the two. So we let Flash and the pony play themselves out.

The afternoon sun was sinking by the time the two equines had finally torn their eyes from one another long enough to think about their stomachs. Tom shook the sweet feed in the dish, attracting their attention. Flash and his new friend looked a bit sheepish about their romantic romp as they followed Tom back to the pasture, neither one daring to meet our eyes.

Once inside the pasture, the little pony shied away at our attempts to remove the old leather halter she wore. It was far too small, and the strap across her nose had rubbed into her flesh, leaving an open wound. Taking it off would have to wait for another day.

"What do you think we should do now?" I asked Tom as we set out hay and filled the trough with fresh water.

"Well, we can't keep her, so don't get any ideas, Rachel," he warned. "And don't give me that look."

"What look?" I tilted my head and blinked several times. Something was tickling my eyelid, and it made my lower lip extend a tiny bit. Occasionally that just happened. I didn't know what Tom was talking about—sometimes he said crazy stuff.

Tom narrowed his eyes and wagged his finger at my face without a word.

We proceeded to temporarily wire the broken fence back together so the duo would stay corralled for the night. At the house, we began making calls to neighbors, animal control, the sheriff's department, and local feed stores. No one had reported losing a brown pony with a white blaze on her face. Just as we had experienced with Flash, history was repeating itself.

∧ ∧

Weeks passed with no response to our flyers. To be honest, I really didn't want to return the mare to someone who had left a tiny halter on her so long that it scarred her delicate nose. Someone who never cared enough to teach her to eat from their hand, who had never trimmed her feet, probably didn't want her back. After a while I gave up looking for the owner and didn't make any effort to find a new home. We simply let the little pony stay.

One morning, Tom and I walked along the mostly over-grown dirt roadway that wound around the inside of the pasture toward the woods at the back. That spring had been stressful as we tried to balance keeping two boats afloat: maintaining enough art and creative design projects until a new business venture could sustain us, and building the new business to the point we could let the art phase out. There was always either too much to do or not enough, and we needed time outside both worlds to calmly regroup.

The road turned past a stand of cedar trees, revealing a small clearing near the woods. Flash and his new companion were grazing in the dewy grass, and we approached them slowly.

Tom pulled a carrot from his pocket and placed it in his palm, crouching low and holding it out for the shy pony. Flash seemed to give her a nod, as if encouraging her to take it, then busied himself with the tallest grasses, pretending not to care whether she would accept the offering. She stepped forward cautiously and stopped just beyond Tom's reach, debating, her nostrils twitching. She stretched her neck as far as it would go, but she was short of the carrot by several inches.

I held my breath. Tom remained motionless. Then I heard his soft voice: "It's okay, little lady. It's okay."

With one last tentative step, her nose touched Tom's hand and sniffed the carrot. Somewhere in her timid self she found courage to grasp the treat and pull it into her mouth. At the first crunch, she blinked with delight at the tasty reward.

Without taking his eyes off her, Tom asked, "Should we call her Penny?"

A speck of dust must have flown into my eye at that moment and made me tear up. But any way you slice it, it was pretty sweet.

Penny's feet looked bad. Her hooves were long and misshapen and far past due for a trim. I called Mr. Jacobs, a local farrier, and explained we had an untamed pony who needed a pedicure. He came the following week to work on both animals.

With a properly fitting halter now gently placed on her head, Tom held Penny's face and quietly reassured her the procedure wouldn't hurt. As Mr. Jacobs clipped and filed Penny's overgrown hooves, she trembled nervously but cooperated admirably throughout the process.

"Now let's take a look at Flash's feet," Mr. Jacobs said, moving his tools a few feet over. "Did you have his hooves trimmed recently?"

"Nope," I said. "It's been almost a year."

"Well, these look pretty good! All they need is a little shaping," Mr. Jacobs said.

"Donkeys' hooves are softer than horses' hooves," Mr. Jacobs continued, his voice raised over the rasping sound of the file. "It's pretty amazing how their hooves stay in good condition when they are able to walk a lot. You can tell the terrain in his pasture is pretty hard and rocky. It keeps these babies naturally shipshape!"

"Well, he's always foraging, so I guess that keeps him moving," I said with a tinge of pride. *My donkey has naturally well-shaped hooves. How many people can say that?*

Mr. Jacobs's eyes wandered around the barn and fell on some chunks of white rock that were lined up against the wall. These weren't just any rocks; they were treasures—fossils Tom had been collecting from our property. Clam-type shells and rocks with shell imprints were by far the most common finds, and it was always exciting when we'd stumble across one.

Recently, pieces of a large fossilized nautilus-shaped shell had been discovered by none other than Flash! His favorite roll spot, smack in the middle of the dirt floor in the three-sided barn, was the site of this buried treasure. Flash's method of rolling from side to side with complete abandon had thrown the top layers of dirt out in all directions, revealing the layer of rock beneath. Each day after his roll he would break off pieces of the rock when he tossed his hooves out front to get up. The shell, an ammonite, had circular ridges that coiled beautifully into the center. Pieced together, it was a good nine inches across.

"I see you got some fossils there," Mr. Jacobs said appreciatively. "This area is loaded with 'em. We actually discovered dinosaur fossils when I had a septic tank put in." He lifted his cowboy hat and wiped his brow. "Whoo-eee, that'll make ya think," he said with a chuckle.

Tom looked at me out of the corner of his eye, one eyebrow raised, while I busied myself adjusting Flash's halter. *Goodness, this strap is mashing your hair down, Flash. That'll never do.*

The truth was, although I marveled at our small finds,

Flash's accidental unearthing of these fossils had made me feel quite uncomfortable. An online search to learn more left me disconcerted when I read that ammonites and other aquatic fossils were eighty to a hundred million years old.

I rejected the assertions. Geologists claiming that Texas was once beneath a sea during the Cretaceous period? It didn't jibe with everything I'd been taught about Creation, and it was easiest not to think about it.

That was before Tom, in an effort to help fortify Grayson against what we felt would be a secular worldview taught in college, had amassed a fair-sized collection of books on geology and nature. I'd been reading over Tom's shoulder as he devoured them, and I found my interest not only piqued but also challenged as I was presented with information that was new to me.

Tom responded to Mr. Jacobs. "Not only are there dinosaur and sea-creature fossils in the different layers around here, but more recent animals too. Did you hear about the fully intact mammoth skeleton that was dug up out of a gravel pit in our county? It's been donated to the Perot Museum of Nature and Science, and I understand it's about twenty to forty thousand years old."

Their conversation continued while I stood next to Flash and stroked his head. He was listening too.

Mr. Jacobs set Flash's hoof down and inspected the partial ammonite shell Tom handed him. Together we admired the detailed protruding bumps and tiny crevices that had decorated a beautiful marine home for an ancient creature.

Open our eyes to behold
thy gracious hand in all thy works . . .

I was in awe.

It's funny—and humbling—when you realize just how little you know about a subject. It ignites curiosity about everything else around you. The geology and nature book collection had led to *more* books: books about cosmology, physics, biology, and theology. Everything they presented told me something new about God. I'd always loved the natural world, and I'd always felt connected to God in a special way while outdoors appreciating His handiwork. I was hooked—and also . . . spiritually conflicted.

I realized that somewhere along the way, I had stopped *learning*. Not intentionally, of course. Life was just so full of responsibilities and activities that I couldn't add one single thing to it, or so I thought. My reading diet consisted of blogs, news headlines, and books on Christian living by popular Christian authors. Oh, I did some Bible studies, but they were topical in nature. I was beginning to see that even my understanding of Scripture was self-curated to maintain a comfortable level of certainty.

I couldn't remember the last time I'd asked serious questions or changed my mind about anything. I couldn't remember ever really seeking out any *new* ideas to inform my thoughts. Somehow, I'd equated "growth" with becoming more convinced about the views I already held.

The more I read—and the more Tom read aloud to me when we crawled into bed at night—the more humbled I became. Just like people I knew who'd made a lot of assumptions about donkeys but had never actually met one in real life, I found that getting up close and poring over books about this wonderful world revealed assumptions I, too, had made in my immense ignorance of even the most basic facts.

I was simply not prepared for the beautiful, thoughtful approach to the natural world by Bible-believing Christians who held different views on Creation than I did. It challenged me to take another look at my paradigm that held science and faith in conflict. Dr. Francis Collins, a world-renowned scientist and committed Christian, said something powerful that stuck with me:

> I do not believe that the God who created all the universe, and who communes with His people through prayer and spiritual insight, would expect us to deny the obvious truths of the natural world that science has revealed to us, in order to prove our love for Him.

I knew I was being invited to take a closer look at nature and the Bible and ask if there was room for the beauty, poetry, and magnificence I saw in creation now that I had allowed myself to move beyond a rigid dichotomy between faith and science. My imagination was ignited with wonder.

All because a donkey had kicked up a fossil.

"Well, looks like Flash and Penny are good to go." Mr. Jacobs turned and gave Flash's rump a pat, causing dust particles to float around his thick fingers. "They sure make quite a pair," he said with a smile.

I thought so too. I untied Penny from the post and removed her halter. She was eager to be free of confines and paraded away on her freshly pedicured feet.

While Tom settled up with Mr. Jacobs for his services, I took Flash's rope and led—er, "encouraged"—him with a handful of sweetgrass in front of his nose. It worked like a charm.

Once we were moving forward at a steady pace toward the south pasture, I allowed the rope to slacken and relaxed into the walk. Flash stayed just behind me, the warmth from his head reassuring on the back of my arm. I had recently memorized a verse from Romans, and the words fell into rhythm with the steady clop-clop-clop of Flash's feet on the rocky trail.

Ever since the world was created, people have seen the earth and sky. Through everything God made, they can clearly see his invisible qualities—his eternal power and divine nature. So they have no excuse for not knowing God.

ROMANS 1:20

Clop-clop-clop. The scent of wild honeysuckle was nearly intoxicating, and I couldn't help but stop to admire the flowering vines scrambling over the fence and reaching for the sun with their delicate blooms. Buttery-colored flowers with golden stamens lured bees to their nectar and passersby such as Flash and me to their fragrance. Breathing deeply and lingering in the scent, I became heady with joy.

Rejoicing in thy whole creation . . .

God created a world so full of the wonder rampantly displayed on these untamed vines. It made perfect sense to reflect on the Divine Being who had brought it into existence. I looked at the expanse of Texas wildflowers in Flash's field—a quilt of yellow, orange, purple, and red blossoms—all growing from hard clay formed on an ocean floor so long ago. *Surely God wasn't trying to trick us by creating a world that only "looks" old, was He?* Maybe God *did* take eons and eons of time to fashion this wonderland we think of as *our pasture.* The idea made me shiver in awe.

I remembered how the Book of Job expounded on the natural world and its animals:

> Just ask the animals, and they will teach you.
>   Ask the birds of the sky, and they will tell you.
> Speak to the earth, and it will instruct you.
>   Let the fish in the sea speak to you.
>
> JOB 12:7-8

After Job had pondered God's role in his many sufferings, the Lord finally revealed Himself by listing aspects of nature and creatures that display His power and wisdom. (I'm happy to report that donkeys made the list!) Job responded, completely undone:

> I know that you can do anything,
>   and no one can stop you. . . .
> I had only heard about you before,
>   but now I have seen you with my own eyes.
>
> JOB 42:2, 5

From what I could tell from the passage, Job did not actually see God's *physical* being, but saw Him *through all that He had made* and was humbled to the point of awestruck silence.

That's when it clicked in my head. *You want to be found, don't you, God? You have created this world in such a way that we will discover You if we release our human tendency to try putting Your handiwork into a box.*

Perhaps all these years that I'd struggled to meet God in prayer, frustrated in my personal defeat, I had missed an easy clue found not just in Job but also throughout Scripture: Go where God's fingerprints are most clearly visible—*in nature*. It was here that I was most open to wonder, to awe . . . to God.

Flash browsed the tender leaves of a willow tree that leaned over the fence while I closed my eyes for one last inhale. I let my breath out slowly—*whooosh*——and with it, somehow, went my fear of the unknown; all fear of the questions I'd avoided was simply gone. I sensed there was nothing I could learn or read or discover that would lead me away from a God who beckons us to come, to taste, to see.

The Bible itself invites us to experience a God who is bigger than any words can describe Him. "Don't be afraid," Jesus said. *Come, delight in all that I have made.*

CHAPTER 5

What We've Left Undone

Most merciful God,
we confess that we have sinned against you
in thought, word, and deed,
by what we have done,
and by what we have left undone.
We have not loved you with our whole heart;
we have not loved our neighbors as ourselves.
We are truly sorry and we humbly repent.
For the sake of your Son Jesus Christ,
have mercy on us and forgive us;
that we may delight in your will,
and walk in your ways,
to the glory of your Name. Amen.

Daily Morning and Evening Prayer: Rite Two,
"Confession of Sin," *The Book of Common Prayer*

F lash was head over hooves in love with Penny.

Anyone could see that.

The small pony's thick winter coat had shed, revealing her smooth summer hair and delicate legs that had been hidden beneath it. Flash and Penny were inseparable now. He followed her everywhere, giving up his bachelor ways of keeping his trails meticulously maintained and pooping in perfect piles. Now, his trails were rarely used, and manure was everywhere. Penny brought a mess of creative force to Flash's previously rhythmed life, but he did not seem to mind one bit.

As the months went on and summer gave way to autumn, we realized there was a baby on the way. We watched Penny's belly grow ever so slowly and began to get excited that we would soon see what their baby mule looked like.

Late one evening, Tom was in the office paying bills. "Hey, we should probably get the vet out here to take a look at Penny and get her vaccinations done," I remarked, bringing him a glass of Dr. Pepper.

He looked at me over his +1.50 readers. "Can it wait?" he asked, motioning to the stack. "I'd rather just take care of all that when the foal arrives so we don't need to have the vet come out twice. She'll be fine."

"I suppose so," I replied, making a mental note to pick up some vaccine injections from A+ Feed. Those shots could be administered without a vet and would cover our bases for now. I still wanted the vet to come out, but seeing Tom's stress, I agreed it could wait. After all, we'd kept Penny from going to the auction block and an unknown fate. *She was lucky to have found her way to us,* I told myself.

∧ ∧

Penny's labor started in late afternoon on a beautiful February day. It seemed a little early by our calculations, but we knew there was some wiggle room in the actual due date. Gestation for horses is generally eleven months, while donkeys take a full twelve. Best we could tell, Penny was right at eleven. We had staked her and Flash in the yard by the house so they could enjoy a change of scenery and the abundant grass outside their pasture.

A thump just outside Tom's office window had interrupted his work. Penny was in the flower bed, kicking the house with her back feet, as if alerting him that contractions had started. We leaped into action, filling her stall with plenty of soft, clean wood shavings; getting water and hay ready; and making sure blankets and towels were on hand. Tom sequestered Flash in the old emu pen and moved Penny into the stall.

A baby mule was on its way!

Unfortunately, the hours ticked by, and we were still waiting at 11 p.m. when a cold front started to move in. With each passing minute, our hopes that the foal might arrive before the temperature plunged all but diminished. Our three-sided barn is far from warm in freezing weather.

Penny kicked her back feet with each contraction, not knowing what else to do with the strange pains she was experiencing. Our vet assured us on the phone that a first-time mom might have a long labor like this. Tom pulled out an arctic sleeping bag so he could keep vigil for the night near the stall. I smiled at Tom as he hand-fed Penny some hay and coaxed her through another contraction. Then I headed indoors for some sleep.

My ringing cell phone woke me.

"She's pushing." Tom's voice alerted every part of me. The sun was barely up as I threw on layers of clothes, grabbed gloves, and poured coffee into a thermal cup. I reached the stall just as the foal's feet began to emerge from Penny's body, then continued watching in utter rapture at this baby mule coming into the world.

A final push and it was here—a tangle of long legs and wet body encased in a semiopaque membrane that steamed in the frigid barn. Penny lay exhausted on the wood shavings. After giving her a few minutes to collect herself, Tom gave her a gentle nudge toward the mule. "Up you go, Penny!" He broke the birth sac open so the little one could breathe.

"Oh my goodness, just look at him!" I whispered, tears of joy streaming down my face. "He is beautiful!" His curly hair was dark brown, but he had the telltale light-colored muzzle of a donkey, and the size of his fuzzy ears was somewhere between long donkey ears and short horse ears—perfectly symmetrical for a mule. His little hooves were tipped with a soft coating of rubbery keratin that had prevented their sharp edges from tearing the birth sac while in Penny's womb.

"Go meet your baby!" I urged Penny, excited for her to begin mothering. Without even glancing at the foal, Penny wobbled off with her head down to the other side of the stall, breathing heavily.

Tom's eyes met mine. *Something isn't right.* My heart thudded in my chest as we cleaned and dried the baby, wrapping him in blankets to keep him warm. Penny kept her distance from the three of us.

"This baby is a preemie," Dr. Howard pronounced after a quick look within minutes of arriving. "If you have any hope of saving him, you'll need to get him to the equine hospital right away and get him on some formula. But even if he starts eating right away, his lungs aren't fully developed. There's a fifty-fifty chance he won't make it." Tom ran to get the Suburban and pull it around to the barn.

My knees started to shake. *This is a life-or-death situation.*

Dr. Howard turned his attention to Penny. He admitted he was puzzled by her behavior, but he did consider the possibility of her inexperience. "Sometimes mamas reject their babies, and we just don't know why," he said. "Let's keep an eye on her over the next twenty-four hours. But first we need to see what can be done for the baby. I'll call ahead to the hospital and let them know you're coming."

The nearest equine hospital was at a horse racetrack thirty long minutes away. Every minute counted now since every minute without colostrum meant serious trouble. While I made sure Penny had fresh food and water in the stall until we returned, Tom picked up the bundled newborn and kissed the top of his silky head. "Hang in there, little prince," he whispered.

Tom gently placed him in the back of the Suburban, and I climbed in beside the foal. I was barely settled when Tom jumped into the driver's seat, threw the vehicle into drive, and gunned it across the pasture to the gate.

I'm pretty sure Tom ran at least two red lights en route to the hospital—at least that's how many I was aware of. He moved just as fast when we arrived, bursting through the front door with the precious patient. The staff members parted like the Red Sea to make way for them, and Tom was motioned into an exam room just beyond the main area where horses were examined. When he carefully unwrapped the mule, everyone fussed over the adorable little creature. A glimpse of the gigantic thoroughbred tethered in the center room made him seem even smaller and more fragile than ever.

A young equine vet took over. "Hi, I'm Dr. Betsy," she said, introducing herself. She held a pen over her clipboard. "Name of animal?"

I looked at Tom.

"Prince," he said, clearing his throat.

Dr. Betsy smiled. "Aww. We'll get Prince hooked up to an IV and order some formula for him." She seemed encouraged as she watched the mule look around the room inquisitively. "We'll monitor his breathing and hope that his lungs are able to keep working."

That lung thing again. My head hurt thinking about it, and yet for the first time that morning, my breathing slowed and my anxiety dissipated. *Prince is in good hands. They will give him the best care.*

"This is the first baby mule we've ever had here," Betsy said. "I think everyone is in love with him already." She gave us her card with her direct phone number. "I will keep you updated on Prince's condition."

Tom stifled a yawn.

"You've been up all night," I said, patting his cheek. I reached for the keys in his coat pocket. "Let's go. I'll drive us home."

When we got back to the barn, Penny seemed calm. She was standing near her hay and looked alert, so Tom and I went inside to get some much-needed sleep.

The next morning, Tom went to the pen to check on Flash, then made a beeline for the barn. Penny was still having occasional involuntary muscle spasms, so Tom walked her around to see if that might help. He videotaped her having another spasm and texted it to Dr. Howard.

A few hours later, Dr. Howard called. "Tom, I think I might know what's making her kick like that. It's really rare in horses—almost unheard of."

"Go ahead. I'm listening."

Dr. Howard took a deep breath. "Well, I doubt this is it, but it could be . . . rabies."

Tom nearly dropped the phone.

Rabies?

Dr. Howard explained. "As you know, rabies vaccinations are not required for equines in Texas, and they have to be administered by a veterinarian. The over-the-counter shots many horse and donkey owners use are effective for West Nile virus, tetanus, and influenza, but they're taking their chances on rabies . . ." His voice trailed off; then he cleared his throat. "If Penny isn't up to date on her rabies shot, that could be what's happening."

Tom suddenly felt weak and had to sit down. "Dear God. I don't know her history before she came to us. She hasn't had her rabies shot since she's been here. We were going to have you do it when you came out for the baby."

"Well, like I said, it's highly unlikely. Last year I think there were only about twenty-five cases out of maybe ten million horses in the country. I've personally never seen it, and neither have any of the other veterinarians I know."

"How could she have gotten it?"

"Rabies is mostly carried by skunks, raccoons, and bats. A rabid one can attack another animal, or even humans for that matter."

There was a long pause as the words sank in.

"On the other hand, Penny's condition might be from nerve damage she suffered during labor. We'll just have to see what happens." Dr. Howard paused. "But just in case it is rabies, you need to keep Flash in his pen and Penny in the stall. Make sure nobody has access to either of them. Rabies is deadly serious, and the animals must be quarantined straightaway. Don't touch them, and don't let anyone else near them. I'll be there as quickly as I can."

I was shattered by the news.

Our frantic Google search yielded horrifying results—rabies is *always* fatal in animals who are infected, and it's almost always fatal in humans if not treated quickly. People and animals who have been exposed to the virus must follow specific protocols.

That meant us. We'd been handling Penny the past few days.

And Flash had been with her up until labor started.

And what about Prince?

I didn't want to think about it.

Meanwhile, Tom called his dad, Bob, to come over for moral support and to provide extra hands in case we needed them. By the time Dr. Howard arrived, Penny was having full-blown seizures. There was no other choice but to put her down.

While Tom, Bob, and Dr. Howard took care of Penny in the

barn, I stood in the kitchen, my head bowed in utter sorrow and my hands on the counter to keep me from falling. I couldn't bear to be out there.

Oh, dear little Penny.

I did the only thing I could: I bawled my eyes out. When Tom finally came inside, we held each other and cried.

We would have to wait the entire weekend for the test results from Penny's tissue sample. *Surely it's some kind of nerve damage from labor that caused all this,* we told ourselves. *Everything will be fine, just fine. Prince will survive, and Flash will . . . oh, dear God, let Flash be okay. Please let him be okay. Please, God.*

The clock was ticking for Tom and me to get medical treatment too, if Penny indeed had rabies. When I began running a fever on Sunday, our fear was palpable. Had I come in contact with any of her bodily fluids? I couldn't remember. Was this fever a fluke? A psycho-illness I had brought on myself? We would need to be at a hospital the moment we got word. Since there is no test for rabies in humans, a positive result for the animal in question meant vaccines would need to be administered right away to anyone who'd been in contact.

We had assumed any emergency room would have what we needed to begin treatment. As it turned out, there was only one hospital in the Dallas area with the postexposure prophylaxis vaccine. On Monday morning, we headed there—before we had even heard from the Texas Department of State Health Services.

Tom's phone rang just as we approached the hospital doors, and he put the call on speakerphone so I could hear.

"Mr. Ridge?"

"Yes."

"I need to inform you that the test for rabies for, uh—" there was a shuffle of papers—"Penny . . . yes, Penny . . . came back positive. Positive for rabies."

"Okay, okay. Thank you." Tom closed his eyes and sank to the curb. "Wait. What do we do now? Is there someone I'm supposed to contact about our donkey being exposed?"

"Yeah, there's an office out in West Texas that covers that protocol, and it's overseen locally by your sheriff. Your vet will need to administer some heavy-duty rounds of vaccinations on your donkey, and then you're required to quarantine the animal for ninety days in a state-approved facility. If you have a pen you can hold him in for that amount of time, you'll have to get it inspected and approved." He paused, then added, "This needs to be done immediately, of course. Otherwise, that donkey will have to be put down too."

"Yes, sir. I understand."

"And listen, anyone who has had contact with the deceased animal, particularly with her saliva, will need to seek medical treatment right away."

Tom thanked him and hung up the phone.

We were both shaking when we entered the hospital and began filling out the admissions paperwork.

^ ^

If only. If only we'd done things differently. If only I'd insisted on having the vet come out earlier . . .

If only. It wasn't the first time in my life I'd said those words, but it had never been more emotional. Our neglect, *my* neglect—there was no other word for it—cost Penny her life. I couldn't really blame Tom. The animals' health care was squarely in my realm of responsibility: I was the partner who kept their feed monitored, their deworming schedule current, and their veterinary needs taken care of. My decision to delay a vet appointment put Prince and Flash—and Tom and me—in grave danger.

We racked our brains trying to make a list of everyone we could think of who might have come in contact with Penny in the previous weeks. Our dear neighbors, Steve and Bridgette? Any children who had visited? We could only think of Bob, who had helped at the end. He, too, would need to seek treatment.

Very expensive treatment. Three rounds of it.

The barn, the stall, and the equipment had to be cleaned and sanitized. Clothing and tack destroyed.

But it was the worry that weighed most heavily.

And the guilt.

The awfulness of everything made me physically ill.

I wasn't prepared for the next phone call, this time from Betsy at the equine hospital.

"I'm so sorry," she choked out the words. "Prince . . . his lungs . . . he didn't make it."

It's all my fault.

It's all my fault.

I knew the importance of that initial vet visit, and yet I didn't insist.

Prince, our beautiful baby mule, the little one I'd had such hopes for, was gone.

No! No! No!

He had fought so hard, and it looked like he was going to turn the corner. Just hours before, Betsy had texted a photo of him standing on his own.

And now he, too, was gone.

I began to hyperventilate, and my vision seemed to go dark. I sank into a chair as my knees turned to jelly.

It's all my fault.

> *. . . by what we have done,*
> *and by what we have left undone.*

I couldn't go back and fix it; I had to live with the consequences of my inaction.

For now, Flash would be stuck in the emu pen—if it passed inspection.

Quarantined for ninety days . . . if he survives.

I wouldn't be able to touch him, scratch his ears, or feed him by hand.

This can't be happening.

I don't know if you've ever relived moments in your past, moments when you made a wrong decision and wished you could go back and undo it. You try to put it out of your mind, but it haunts you. You review all the reasons you did what you did: You were doing the best you could; you were rushed and didn't have time to carefully think it through; you had good intentions; no one is perfect—everyone makes mistakes.

You tell yourself to move on.

But you can't.

You can't push past your mistake, in part because you know you deserve all the consequences and judgment. You say over and over, "I *knew* better."

I was probably in my twenties when someone told me it's

not the things you *do* in life that you'll regret—it's what you *don't* do. The chances you don't take, the love you don't give, the good you don't do for others. Those are the things you'll regret.

At the time, I was so full of youthful arrogance that I quickly thanked the person, then thought sarcastically, *I'll log that away . . . for never.* I would be that one person in the entire history of the world who would never not do everything they intended. I would live without regrets. As newlyweds, Tom and I even made a pinky promise: "No regrets," we said.

Who were we kidding? We both regretted things we had done in order to *not* have the regrets in the first place.

But then there is the matter of letting go of those regrets. You know it's not healthy to stay stuck in them. You *know* you need to forgive yourself.

Time has taught me that usually it is much easier to forgive others for their shortcomings than it is to forgive yourself for your own. It's easier to walk away from others' wrongs than to leave yours behind.

It's the things we've left *undone* that haunt us—that haunt me.

Often it's because those are the things that, even with the best of intentions, get lost in the shuffle of everyday life. In our busyness, we just forget to follow through. No one would likely ever know, because who else knows what we *should* have done?

Other times, we choose to deliberately skirt responsibilities or acts of goodness by taking an easier way out. It seems like the path of least resistance is the path I follow best.

But this thing with Penny . . . this one huge mistake of mine seemed to snowball into a tangled mess with every other thing I'd ever done wrong, and I found myself drowning in regrets, sinking in self-recrimination—big and small, important (Why didn't I finish college? Why didn't I stand up for my child when an adult said something unkind? How could I have gone back on a promise to a friend?) and unimportant (Why didn't I use sunscreen on my hands? Why did I wear such voluminous clothing in the eighties?). I regretted everything.

Why didn't I insist the vet come out when I knew it was the right thing to do?

Because, well . . . because I always choose the easy thing. The thing that doesn't create conflict in the moment.

It's my MO in a nutshell.

Ugh.

Even now, a few years removed from the tragedy of Penny and Prince and the danger I put others in, I find it difficult to think about. I feel the sadness to this day. I did not want to write about this and hoped I could fast-forward to greener pastures.

But life is messy. It doesn't fold on the dotted lines and become a Hallmark card with carefully crafted sentiments and pretty pictures.

Some things can't be rushed through, and this was going to be one of them.

It was hard to find words to pray, so mostly I didn't.

I couldn't pray, not even outside in nature like I had wanted to do before all this happened.

The best I could do was *read* a prayer. I could sit on the couch and read the words through a blur of tears.

I found my way to the "Confession of Sin."

Most merciful God . . .
we have sinned against you
in thought, word, and deed . . .

In my place of defeat, this is what I wanted—words to express what my soul was feeling.

I grew up with a form of faith, reflected in the words of our prayers, that was always eager to find victory in every circumstance. I was good at *thanking* God for forgiveness and being able to "come boldly before the throne," after which I'd move on to "claim the promises."

Don't get me wrong—I'm ever so grateful for the call to look upward, to find the blessing, to stand on the Word. I know it's important, and I wouldn't trade it.

I realized in this moment, though, that I'd missed something along the way. I'd missed my own very human need to lament and confess. My personal practice of prayer, as inconsistent as it was, was composed of words such as "Lord, I just want to thank You for _____ and ask You for _____ and _____ . . ."

There was a lot of requesting involved, and to be fair, I'm sure God didn't mind. But I was cheating my soul of the necessity of dealing with the real, raw stuff going on in my life. I glossed over those damaged parts almost as if they weren't important, thinking maybe they'd only serve to take my focus off claiming the victory. My system was faulty, reminiscent of the time I painted the wainscoting in our living room without priming first. The end result looked wonderful . . . until you scratched the surface and, lacking the right preparation underneath, the paint peeled off in sheets. As long as you never really bumped it, the finish was *totally* fine.

Confession, it turns out, is really good for the soul, laying a foundation for our prayer life to flourish and opening our hearts to receive God's mercy.

And how we need His mercy. How I need His mercy.

Most merciful God . . .

Did you know that His mercies never end—they are new every morning?

They are. I have found this to be true.

When you find yourself, as I did, overwhelmed with regrets and unable to forgive yourself, know there *is* healing in the merciful arms of Jesus. Confession is not about beating yourself up or about giving your shortcomings to God so *He* can beat you up. Neither is it a brief formality in a system of prayer designed to make you a more successful Christian.

No, regular confession creates a posture of humility, a space that allows the Holy Spirit to gently remind you of shortcomings and the opportunity to listen for His conviction. It lays your soul bare and exposes your wounds so that God can pour the healing balm of His mercy upon them. You just need to keep coming back and coming back, giving them to Him and giving them to Him . . . as long as it takes you. There's no rush, no timetable for healing.

He already knows all.

He has already forgiven all.

And He understands all. He knows it might take us, in our

human frailty, some time to receive His mercy in its full extravagance.

I couldn't fix this. I couldn't go back in time and change what had happened. I could only go forward, trusting that my most merciful God was ever present, ever caring, and ever forgiving.

CHAPTER 6
This New Day

Lord God, almighty and everlasting Father,
you have brought us in safety to this new day:
Preserve us with your mighty power,
that we may not fall into sin,
nor be overcome by adversity;
and in all we do,
direct us to the fulfilling of your purpose;
through Jesus Christ our Lord. Amen.

Daily Morning Prayer: Rite Two, "A Collect for Grace,"
The Book of Common Prayer

sat outside Flash's pen by the hour, watching for any telltale symptoms of rabies:

Is he kicking his back foot, or is he just trying to shoo the flies?

Is he drooling, or did he just drink water?

Does he look lethargic?

What's wrong with his ears?

Why is he walking around?

How come he's just standing there?

Ninety days of quarantine for rabies exposure.

Ninety days of worry.

Ninety days of praying, "Oh, God, please. Please, don't let him die."

What if he dies?

Flash pressed his nose up against the eight-foot-high chain-link fence and rubbed his lips on it, his nostrils opened wide. His upper lip got stuck, leaving his teeth exposed in what looked like a wide grin. *Why am I in here instead of out there?*

He tried to cajole me into opening the gate by looking irresistible. He pricked his ears forward, the fuzzy hair wafting in the breeze; then he wiggled them back and forth independently, like a parlor trick. "Oh, baby, you're going to have to stay in there awhile," I murmured. "But we will be here every day."

The old emu pen that sat in the middle of Flash's pasture had passed the sheriff's inspection. Since it was a secure enclosure *within* a secure enclosure (a pasture with good fences and locked gates), we were allowed to keep him on site. Still, this was not going to be easy. I knew Flash wasn't thrilled with his confinement, but it was far better than taking him to a state-run facility, where he would be completely isolated.

Flash's smile faded and his head drooped, as if he couldn't bear to put a brave face on his situation another minute longer. He sighed deeply, his stomach bulging with the inhale and compressing with the exhale. He missed Penny. *Why did she vanish so suddenly, and why am I imprisoned?*

I picked up a long stick and pushed it through the fence to scratch Flash's shoulder. "I'm so sorry about all this, buddy. I never meant for anything bad to happen."

As I fumbled with the stick, I thought back to the previous weekend, when Tom and I had gone to the emergency room to start our rounds of rabies treatments.

It was the same day our younger daughter, Meghan, was scheduled for an ultrasound to learn the gender of her first baby. As we filled out the admission paperwork, I looked at my watch. *She'll be calling us in an hour.*

Although we had shared the drama of the premature labor and Penny's and Prince's passing with our kids, we had not told any of them about the possibility of rabies being the source. We reasoned we didn't want to worry them needlessly if it turned out to be a false alarm. Now we were potentially in real danger from exposure. And yet, I wasn't going to put a damper on Meghan's exciting news. We'd have to keep it secret a little longer.

"We'll put you in examination rooms right next to each

other," the nurse said. "We're just waiting on the serum from the lab downstairs."

I leaned back on the paper-covered exam table and shivered. *It must be 52 degrees in here! I need socks.*

"Are you okay over there?" Tom must have overheard my thoughts.

"Yeah, I'm okay," I said. "I'm just glad we're here, getting treatment."

"I'm sorry about all this." He poked his head in the doorway and gave me a small smile that said everything I needed to know: *We're in this together.*

"This is taking forever. Can I wait with you?" He plopped into the chair and pretended to relax.

I was glad to have his company. In more than three decades of marriage, we had been through a lot together, but this was a first. Getting rabies shots wasn't on our bucket list of adventures to undertake together.

The nurse wheeled her cart in and snapped on her gloves, just as my phone rang.

"Excuse me, but I'm going to have to take this," I told her. "Do you mind waiting outside for a moment?" I put the phone on speaker, and Tom and I leaned over to listen. I closed my eyes to block out our surroundings.

"It's a girl!" Meghan shouted. "We're having a little girl!"

A girl! A baby girl. *Dear Jesus, thank You, thank You, thank You.*

Tom and I cheered while we wiped tears of happiness from our eyes. Meghan's excited voice echoed into the exam room as we began discussing baby names and nursery themes.

"Oh, sweetheart, we are so proud and thrilled for you! We

just can't wait for this little girl to arrive!" I clapped my hands, unable to contain my joy.

After I hung up, Tom and I put our arms around each other for a long moment. There were no words to express the flood of emotions washing over us: the joy of new life, the terror of rabies, the grief over Penny and Prince, the need for each other. Every one of our nerve endings was on alert, heightening every feeling.

"Knock, knock!" The nurse cheerily bustled back in. "Now if you'll both just drop your drawers, I'll inject your right butt cheeks."

You know, when the preacher at our wedding asked us to repeat "Until death do us part," I could not have imagined we would wind up in *this* scenario. But then, what can you imagine when you're nineteen and twenty-two years old? We were a couple of kids in love, fresh out of a small Pentecostal Bible school, with nothing but blue skies and sunshine ahead. I couldn't have foreseen the twists and turns life would take to bring us here.

"Well, I always wanted to get matching tattoos," I said. "I guess this is as close as we'll get."

Tom smiled at me, and lest it seem inappropriate, we both struggled to swallow the laughter that offered a small relief valve for the emotional pressure we were trying to keep inside.

Ahem. Flash's grunt reminded me he didn't care that I was lost in a reverie of thoughts, but please, could I at least keep the stick moving? He maneuvered his body around so that my ad hoc back scratcher could now reach his backside. My own backside was still sore from the rabies shot days earlier. He swayed back and forth with his eyes closed, clearly appreciative of the make-shift massage tool. With small steps, he managed to position himself so he got all his itches scratched. Despite the barrier between us, he made it work.

Finally, Flash seemed satisfied with my service, so I pulled the stick back through the fence and tossed it away. With eyes half-closed, Flash stood motionless except for his tail swishing at a fly. A train horn blew in the distance, so faint you could barely make out the sound. On a quiet night when the wind blows just right, you can hear the train rolling through town, a good ten miles away. I turned and let the south breeze brush my face. *When Flash is freed three months from now, the wind will be heavy with summer heat. The spring wildflowers will be long gone.* Flash loves munching the yellow ones, effectively clearing the entire field. *Next year, buddy.*

That is, *if* he survived.

In all we do, direct us . . .

"Yoo-hoo!" a voice from beyond the pasture called to us. It was our neighbor Bridgette, who seemed to never show up at our house without something in her hands. Sometimes it would be a bowl of her famous Cajun gumbo, sometimes a chocolate bar from a recent trip to an exotic locale, or sometimes a plant from her garden. This time, it was a vintage vase filled with an array of wild blooms, leaves, and grasses gathered from the fields between our homes.

"I thought you could use some cheerin' up, hon," she said, meeting me at the gate and giving me a tight squeeze. Bridgette held out the colorful arrangement, then pulled a card from her pocket. Lettered in her block-style architect's handwriting, the envelope read "Tom & Rachel" and displayed a little heart by our names. I felt my throat constrict.

"Tom told us *every*thing," she said in her Louisiana drawl. I swallowed hard.

"I guess you know I should have—"

Bridgette cut me off. "Shh, now. What's done is done. I know this is hard, but don't you spend another minute beating yourself up. That's not going to help anything."

There is no point in arguing with Bridgette when her mind is made up. A talented architectural designer who runs her own firm, she had been my friend for a decade or more, and I knew her well enough to know when to shut up.

Bridgette is one of my life's best surprises. When we first met, I was so intimidated by her I could barely speak. She seemed to be everything I was not:

She was successful; I was floundering.

She was educated; I never finished college.

She was stylish; I was still wearing Mom jeans.

She was Southern; I was from the north.

She was charming; I was from the north.

She was a multitasker extraordinaire; I was a "unitasker," struggling with one thing at a time.

"How's Hay-soos doing?" Bridgette looked over my shoulder to the pen; Flash gazed back, longing for freedom.

Hay-soos, the Spanish pronunciation of *Jesus*, was the pet name she had given Flash when she first saw him. At first the nickname irritated me to no end, but now it warmed my heart. Yes, Bridgette and I had come far over the years. After my initial hesitation to get to know her, we began collaborating on projects together, and my intimidation melted when I learned just how kind and genuine she was.

"Listen, I've got a new project I'd like you to take a look at," Bridgette said. "Do you have a minute? I'd like to show you some plans for a development Steve and I are working on that will start next year. We sure could use your ideas."

I knew what she was up to. She was trying to get me to engage in something other than worry. We went inside the house, where she flipped through drawings and made a few sketches here and there, her familiar drawl soothing.

Her strategy was working, at least temporarily. With everything going on, I welcomed a new creative project to occupy the edges of my mind. I tried to push down my anxiety about Flash's well-being, but I knew I wouldn't sleep well for the duration of the ninety days.

∧ ∧

Each morning, I held my breath as I walked to Flash's pen, afraid of what I might find. Would he be kicking or drooling or lying down? Each morning, he greeted me with The Look: *Let me outta here!*

Exhale, Rachel. I'd throw a ration of hay into the pen, fill the water bucket, and then check on him throughout the day. Most times, I peered from a discreet distance, the way you look in on a baby from the hallway as she plays in her crib. If the baby catches sight of you, she starts fussing and wants to be picked up, when only a moment before she was contentedly gazing at her fingers or grasping her toes.

It was the same with Flash. I was always relieved to see

him stripping leaves from the trees in his pen, giving himself a rollicking dirt bath, or rubbing his bum against a fence post. He seemed content as long as he didn't see me. If he caught a glimpse of me, he'd head straight to the gate and start wheezing a prebellow to make his jail-break wishes known. It was torture to leave him there alone, looking so pathetic. I avoided this whole dramatic scene as much as possible by peeking around the corner of the barn, looking for movement and listening for sounds of trouble. If Flash didn't notice me, I'd tiptoe away, happy that he was alive another day.

Meanwhile, regular life had to go on. Hamburger needed to be thawed in time for dinner. Bathrooms needed cleaning. Laundry refused to do itself. One day as I folded clothes in the bedroom, I turned on my favorite BBC show, *Escape to the Country*, in which prospective home buyers in Great Britain look for country properties. I reached in the basket for a shirt, happy to be transported to gorgeous Wales. *Oh, those thatched roofs!*

Out of the blue, my heart started pounding, and I shivered as beads of sweat dotted my forehead. I was getting woozy— a rush of overwhelming worry and fear seemingly taking over my body. I couldn't think straight; everything was jumbled. I felt for the edge of the bed and sat down, closing my eyes and gulping deep breaths. I'm not sure how long it lasted—maybe only a minute or two—but it paralyzed me with its power.

I used to roll my eyes at people who said they experienced anxiety attacks, thinking that all they needed was to pull themselves together. *Dear Lord, forgive me for my ignorance.*

Anxiety is real.

The very real and intense anxiety-filled moments I experienced were infrequent enough that I didn't seek medical help. But for some, it should not be taken lightly. The condition can be debilitating, requiring medication and professional assistance.

My anxiety was mostly a low-level, constant hum of *What if?*

I was anxious not only about Flash but also about *all* the *What ifs?* in life.

What if I get sick?

What if something happens to one of our children?

What if something happens and we can't pay our bills?

What if I have a flat tire on a busy freeway?

What if I choke on a ham sandwich?

What if I get caught in a flash flood? (my ultimate nightmare)

What if the house burns down?

What if my marriage fails?

What if I haven't read my Bible enough?

What if I haven't prayed enough?

What if I've missed my calling?

What if I've missed God?

What if I'm wrong about everything?

What if?

It was like a virus had taken hold. With a virus, most of the time you don't even know you've been infected until the symptoms show up. Seeing Flash sequestered, going through the rounds of shots with Tom (thankfully the subsequent shots were in our arms), and waiting out these three months forced me to think about everything on a deeper level. I didn't have much of a choice.

Worry begins as tiny cells that morph and multiply into mutants running amok in your mind. These mutants tell you every situation in your life is doomed. Anxiety begins to scribble all over everything with a dark, messy crayon, then crumples up the page. *What's the point of even trying? It's all going to be a disaster.*

Anxiety had shoved me into a funk. I'd fought it on and off before, but now it was a full-on battle. What I needed right then—mentally and spiritually—was a heavy-duty vaccination and a quarantine.

I needed new self-talk and soul care. On a practical level, I needed rest and good food and time with friends like Bridgette. It's not easy to admit weakness, especially when you think it's all in your head. Bridgette's kindness was a healing balm; sometimes something as simple as eating her homemade cheesy potatoes, when it wasn't even a holiday, ministered comfort to my soul.

But spiritually, I was bone-dry. Praying felt impossible. I flailed about in Psalms, which didn't help me; nor did the guilt over my inability to organize my spiritual life when I needed it most. Even in the best of times I'd struggled to maintain a personal devotion time—something that is supposed to be the backbone of a vibrant faith. You'd think I'd have mastered this by now. So not only did the anxiety weigh on me, but my lack of consistency also added to my sense of guilt.

What I needed was a daily liturgy. At the time, I didn't even know what *liturgy* meant. Liturgy is literally "a work of the people," or even better, "a work *for* the people." It's simply an order of worship, laid out long ago, that helps people read, pray, and worship in ways that are constructive and formative.

The Book of Common Prayer gave me something to hang on to. Inside its pages is "The Daily Office," a set of Scripture readings, prayers, and Creeds. Each day I could enter the stream of worship that already seemed to be flowing with or without me. I could let it carry me. There was nothing I needed to make up on my own. I didn't have to decide which book or verse to meditate on. Knowing that I was surrounded by millions of other Christians—all reading, breathing, praying the same things—nourished my weary soul.

I treasured the prayers and Scripture I found each day. As I began to read and participate regularly, I discovered online versions that were easy to pull up on my phone and devices. Some aspects of modern life are really nice! In an instant, I could be buoyed by the strength of the worldwide church.

Each day's reading was a dose of antidote to my anxiety.

With my Bible in one hand and prayer book (or device app) in the other, I began to do more than simply find a comforting prayer here and there; I began to embrace the discipline of having the morning and evening prayers set out for me like a feast—not *instead* of my own prayers, but *alongside* them—to help shape my thoughts and bring me close to the Lord.

*Almighty and everlasting Father, you have
brought us in safety to this new day . . .*

Simply breathing these words made my thoughts focus on Him, dissipating all the anxiety about tomorrow and what *might* happen.

THIS new day.

Today.

I'm safely here.

Jesus is present today. He has brought me here in safety. All I am being asked to do is live in this moment—in this day—in His presence. Rather than my worried, anxious petitions repeating in my head, I now had something I could grab hold of and pray.

He is present with me today. I am safe. As I began to meditate on the reality of those words, I started to sense His presence everywhere.

Beginning my day with liturgy fenced in my anxiety, keeping my mind free from invading mutant cells. My spirit became girded with truth as I joined the ever-flowing stream of prayers, forcing anxiety to play by itself in a corner. I would peek in on it every now and then, but never disturb it—it *always* wanted out. I didn't have to *deny* the anxious thoughts, just refuse to give them power to overtake me.

Each day, I'd simply pray the day's prayers, slowly and out loud.

I'd read the daily Scripture readings. Recite the Creeds.

Let them all continue to do their work in my spirit.

One day at a time.

Worry doesn't always disappear overnight, but how liberating it is to turn our attention only to what is in front of us today. It allows us strength to fight today's battles, love to fill today's needs, and courage to be our truest selves *now*. Today's thing may be a really hard thing, an "impossible" thing, but in this moment, being present before Christ and "the fulfilling of [His] purpose"—through giving, loving, and simply being—is the best that we can do. These words of the psalmist confidently assure us as well:

Where can I go from your Spirit?
   Where can I flee from your presence?
If I go up to the heavens, you are there;
   if I make my bed in the depths, you are there.
If I rise on the wings of the dawn,
   if I settle on the far side of the sea,
even there your hand will guide me,
   your right hand will hold me fast.

PSALM 139:7-10, NIV

CHAPTER 7
People of His Pasture

Come, let us sing to the Lord;
let us shout for joy to the Rock of our salvation.
Let us come before his presence with thanksgiving
and raise a loud shout to him with psalms.

For the Lord is a great God,
and a great King above all gods.
In his hand are the caverns of the earth,
and the heights of the hills are his also.
The sea is his, for he made it,
and his hands have molded the dry land.

Come, let us bow down, and bend the knee,
and kneel before the Lord our Maker.
For he is our God, and we are the people of his pasture
and the sheep of his hand.
Oh, that today you would hearken to his voice!

Daily Morning Prayer: Rite Two, "*Venite*: Psalm 95:1-7,"
The Book of Common Prayer

Day ninety.

"Good to go," Dr. Howard said, giving Flash a final booster shot while we stood inside the pen. It was the first time I'd touched Flash in three months, and my hands were trembling as I held his halter. "Flash is cleared; he doesn't have rabies."

I couldn't contain myself. I jumped up and down from sheer exuberance and threw my arms around Flash.

He had made it. Dear God, he had made it!

"Oh, Flash! You did it!" was all I managed to say as I pressed my face into his neck at long last. He smelled so good and was all dusty and fuzzy and warm—just like I remembered. His eyes sparkled with excitement, as if he couldn't believe his luck at seeing his gate ajar.

"I'm going to brush you and pet you until you can't stand it," I told him. "But not in here." He eagerly followed me into the pasture, lifting his nose to capture every scent wafting on the breeze.

Grooming can definitely wait.

The sky seemed bluer and the wispy clouds whiter that late May morning. Maybe I was imagining it, but even the grass was a brighter shade of green. Some of Flash's favorite yellow flowers had managed to hang around for him to feast on. Tom saw us and joined me outside, putting his arm around my shoulders.

As Flash trotted out into the field, he startled a pair of

roadrunners, who had mistakenly thought they could enjoy their courtship ritual in private. Now they had an audience.

The male roadrunner dangled a fat grasshopper from his beak as a luscious gift for his maiden. She darted away, serpentine style, in apparent disinterest.

"No, it's for *you*!" He craned his head forward and gave chase.

Suddenly, she stopped. Her suitor froze.

Looking over her shoulder, she gave him a coy, "I simply don't care for you" look, then zigzagged her way into the brush as if she were trying to lose him.

Undeterred, he followed her . . . and with a flap of wings, that's just where she caught him. Her hard-to-get act worked beautifully.

Flash's upper lip curled in what appeared to be a smile, clearly savoring an everyday pasture moment—something he had missed during his time in the pen. Then he was off, trotting toward the far end of the pasture. Literally kicking up his heels, he bucked twice in joyful abandon halfway through his run.

"Looks like Flash is happy to be out," Tom said, laughing. He turned me toward him and looked me in the eye. "Are you okay?"

I nodded in relief. "It's been a long three months, hasn't it?"

"If you only knew how many times I checked on Flash, expecting to see him lying there dead." Tom shook his head. "It's so good to see him back in the pasture!"

"I can't wait to walk the trails with him. I couldn't bear to do it alone, knowing he could see me. He wouldn't have understood why he wasn't allowed to be with me."

"I've got the trails mowed and ready for you," Tom said.

"There's just one last thing we need to do." Tom hesitated for a moment. "We, um, we need to let Flash see the spot where Penny passed."

I squeezed my eyes shut for a moment, then peeked at Tom through one of them. "Are you sure? I hate to interrupt Flash's first morning of freedom." I knew Tom was probably right, even if I considered it just a formality. I figured Flash wouldn't really understand what we were trying to show him.

"I think we should do it now, while we're here with him. He'll have lots of time in the pasture, but this is something we should do together." Tom was already pulling an apple slice from his pocket.

I nodded. It was the right thing to do.

"Come on, buddy!" Tom called to him with his "come get a treat" whistle. We waited while Flash reluctantly made his way back, then led him to the barn. To my surprise, he immediately walked into the stall where Penny had last laid, sniffing the layer of fresh wood shavings covering the dirt floor.

"He knows," I whispered. "He knows this is where she was."

Flash circled the space, then stopped and blew hard through his nostrils. He pawed at the shavings to expose the dirt, then placed his nose directly on the cleared ground. Tom took off his cap, and we inched close to the stall, resting our arms on the top rail of the partition. Flash's nostrils flared and constricted with each breath, blowing the dirt and shavings.

The clear notes of a mockingbird's song were caught by the warm breeze and drifted through the open window, a perfect musical accompaniment to the memorial ceremony taking place inside the barn. Flash circled the stall again, stopping at the spot where Penny had been one more time. His ears were slumped as he blinked slowly. The minutes ticked by.

His Penny wouldn't be coming back.

A tear trickled down my cheek; I wiped it from my chin with the back of my hand.

These past three months, Tom and I had been grieving and worrying on our own. Grief, it seems, can only be shared to a certain point—even with those you're closest to. And then it's a solitary burden. No one can work through your emotions for you, or tell you when you're "done," or fix the hole you feel inside. There's a sense of loneliness, sometimes because you don't want to burden the other person at an inopportune moment, and sometimes because it just hurts to talk about it. At times, all Tom and I could do was reach across the space between us and squeeze a hand or nod at one another in a gesture of understanding. *I know this is hard.*

As the last of the bird's song faded away, I realized I had been so anxious about Flash's physical health and my own well-being that it never occurred to me that *he* had suffered a great loss and needed time to grieve too. How did I miss this? I should have known.

How fitting that we were all here together for a last good-bye.

Flash seemed lost in thought. *Is he remembering Penny and the time they had together?*

We watched him move his lips along the ground and sigh. Finally, he turned to leave the stall but paused next to me on his way out, rubbing his head against my shoulder. Then he stood quietly.

People always say the thing they love most about their animals is the way they show unconditional love and endless devotion to their humans. They simply accept you for who you are, wanting to be with you. Flash's gentle demeanor, in the midst of this emotional farewell to Penny, comforted me with a shared sense of peace. There was no judgment, no blame—only love. I put my hands on the sides of that big old noggin, held his face, and pressed my lips to his fuzzy forehead. *Thank you, dear Flash.*

Enough of that. He stepped away and headed toward Tom's worktable. Obviously, my hug had gone too far, making him feel awkward.

Flash surveyed the tools, safety goggles, wood, and supplies. Picking up a glove with his teeth, he shook it and dropped it on the ground. Next came the other glove, followed by the tape measure. It hit the ground with a clank, startling Flash backward into a stack of empty boxes. They scattered everywhere. The unintended crash confused him further, and he tucked his tail and jumped forward. With a small hop to the side, Flash exited the barn before anything else could go wrong.

"He's ba-a-ack!" Tom said with a wry grin.

Despite drying the last of my tears, I had to laugh. I had missed his antics.

Flash headed back toward the field, and I followed him into the sunshine, watching him munch the remaining yellow wildflowers. Breathing deeply, I could only say, "Thank You."

Thank You, Lord.

Words from the *Venite* expanded my prayer:

Come, let us sing to the Lord;

let us shout for joy to the Rock of our salvation.

Let us come before his presence with thanksgiving . . .

Venite is Latin for *Come!*—a liturgical invitation to give thanks and praise to the Lord each morning. Even though a big piece of my heart still ached over all that had happened, I was still extremely grateful.

Okay, I didn't actually shout out loud for joy, but my heart swelled with thankfulness as I stepped into the field before me. I could sense the Lord's presence there, as if the pasture were indeed His court. How appropriate to meditate on these words right here in my own pastoral setting:

> Come, let us bow down, and bend the knee,
> and kneel before the Lord our Maker.
> For he is our God,
> and *we are the people of his pasture* and the sheep of
> his hand.

As I lingered with my thoughts, the wind rustling the grass felt timeless, ancient. Somehow it became the sound of a tent flap opening as a shepherd's household woke to a new day.

It's gonna be another hot one!

Maybe bread was baking on the fire, soon to be eaten with a bit of honey and cheese—strength for a new day of tending sheep.

Did the shepherds of old know which fields grew the choicest grasses and wildflowers? Of course! They lived and breathed the land. Though a relative newcomer to country living, even I know what time of year the thorn trees' leaves are tender and the ryegrass comes up, when the thistles send out their seeds and the dry creek bed might have water. Seasonal changes—some as subtle as a shift in wind direction, the pungent scent of dried locust-tree pods, and the song-filled arrival of robins on their way north—speak to the souls of land dwellers and remind us we are not in control of the universe. Perhaps the best we can hope for is to eke out a livelihood as we become students of our environment and live in gratitude to God.

Pulling an old stump into the shade, I perched on its uneven surface and watched Flash shake his ears and grab another mouthful of grass. It was the perfect setting to continue mulling over what I'd been thinking about during Flash's quarantine:

We are the people of his pasture . . .

What a quaint turn of phrase that now made sense to me. In Scripture, God spoke the language of His people. He interacted with them in their own time and place so they could know Him and learn His ways. Crowds listening to Jesus understood His teaching best when He used familiar imagery that referenced their everyday life: farming, tending sheep, fishing, baking bread, and going to the marketplace.

As ancient people, Jesus' audience clearly thought as their contemporaries did. The ever-changing sky was a solid dome traveled by the sun and moon each day. They viewed the land as a fixed mass standing on pillars, which God in his goodness had given them.

Yet none of their primitive ways of looking at the world fazed Jesus. He met them where they were, accommodating His message in ways they could understand. I was beginning to see that as a modern reader, I needed to step into the pages of history and "try on" the Bible's cultures and languages in order to fully appreciate them.

I'd been learning to read my Bible with fresh eyes, to find the thoughts, ideas, and concepts *behind* the words so I could find meaning there. Since the writers and compilers of Scripture were fully engaged with the natural world and culture of their day, I knew I couldn't always come to the text with my twenty-first-century mind-set that tries to prove everything rationally, scientifically, or even historically.

In the past, I'd been told that every single word in the Bible was factually true and therefore must be taken literally. If even a few tiny things failed to add up, the entire foundation of Christianity would come crashing down. This made for some uncomfortable reading at times, but it also gave me a sense I shouldn't pay attention to details that didn't seem to jibe. Best to pretend you never noticed them in the first place.

When I was a kid, my family and I spent a long, hot summer visiting my grandparents in Nebraska. When it was over, we had a long drive home to Poulsbo, Washington. It was the seventies, and we were a rambunctious preacher's family riding in a '68 New Yorker and pulling a trailer across the open road.

Our trailer wasn't a plush RV with all the amenities, but a utilitarian box on wheels to hold all the things we couldn't fit inside the car, such as family heirlooms from my grandparents and items like tools and a lawn mower that had been picked up at farm sales. My older brother, Eric, and I had proudly emblazoned the silver trailer with evangelistic messages painted in bold, black lettering: Jesus saves. One way. Jesus is coming soon. Evangelism was a family affair, and we figured that between the painted proclamations and the tracts we left behind at every gas station and rest stop, revival would be sparking in our wake.

I'm sure we were quite a sight on the road: Eric, Katherine, and I crammed in the back seat with enough pillows to (hopefully) keep us from invading one another's personal space. Mom and Dad were in the front with my little brother, Dan, propped between them.

No seat belts, of course, but that was actually handy because it allowed us to configure ourselves in different ways as the countryside flew past and our discomfort levels rose. In the back we took turns sitting on the side where the cooler was on the floor, which meant your feet rested on the ice chest and your knees were tucked under your chin.

The other side was more spacious. Sometimes Katherine stacked enough pillows on the floor to equal the height of the hump in the middle, and she would curl up there while I stretched out on the middle of the seat without touching Eric—much. With no air-conditioning, it was important to stay "on your side of the line."

As we crossed the miles for Jesus, I would glance at my parents—Dad, handsome and hip with his muttonchop sideburns and one hand on the wheel, Mom in her '70s denim jumper and cool bandana headscarf. Mom would hand out small paper cups of apple juice (carefully poured from a jug she kept at her feet) and make peanut butter and jelly sandwiches on a cutting board in her lap. We lived for Dairy Queens since there were no McDonald's along the way, and rest areas were few and far between.

My siblings and I passed the time playing the Alphabet Game (a visual race to spot all the letters of the alphabet on signs and license plates), learning to sing harmony in praise songs, and reading Encyclopedia Brown books until we were carsick. This was a no-frills ride but definitely an adventure that made it into the family history books.

Long about Idaho came the highlight of the entire summer. The back seat occupants would have slept right through it had we not suddenly heard . . .

"KIDS! DON'T LOOK!" Mom shouted, jerking us from our slumber. Immediately, we peered out the window. A car was passing us in the left lane, and someone's big ol' bare backside was pressed up against the back seat window. A stranger was mooning us! The driver eased slightly over the centerline, getting even closer, and hung with us for a while before speeding away.

While my parents muttered about what the world was coming to, my siblings and I exchanged wide-eyed glances and mouthed, "Did you *see* that?"

"Kids, you didn't see that, did you?" Mom looked over her shoulder and pointed the butter knife at us.

"What? Nope, nuh-uh. Didn't see it. Did we miss something good?" I tried to look as if I'd been sleeping. It was difficult to keep from grinning, but we all gave her our most convincing expressions, then pretended to settle back to sleep. Katherine and I scrunched down and debriefed in whispers. Yes, indeed, we'd seen it all. Thanks, Mom.

All in all, good times.

A thick reference book had been collecting dust on my desk. I'd pulled *The Big Book of Bible Difficulties* from our personal library some time ago, hoping it would be helpful in my quest to better understand Scripture. The author provides answers to "problematic" issues in the Bible that critics have pinpointed as apparent errors and discrepancies. Although many people might appreciate this approach, it left me troubled. Its concise "nothing to see here" solutions didn't satisfy my inquiries. I stacked other books on top of it for a while, then finally returned it to the bookshelf.

By now I couldn't return to my old approaches to Scripture: Either try to prove everything or simply *pretend* not to see anything conflicting or confusing to my twenty-first-century sensibilities.

But how should I read it?

It was a relief to learn that I could still possess a high view of Scripture by faithfully approaching it through another lens. John Walton, professor of Old Testament at Wheaton College, and Brent Sandy, professor of New Testament and Greek at Wheaton, say this:

> Most of us are probably unprepared . . . for how different the ancient world is from our own. . . . The Old Testament is more similar to the culture of the ancient Near East, and the New Testament to the culture of the Greeks and Romans, than either is to our twenty-first-century world. We're thousands of years and thousands of miles removed. It means we frequently need to put the brakes on and ask whether we're reading the Bible in light of the original culture or in light of contemporary culture. While the Bible's values were very different from the ancient cultures', it obviously communicated in the existing languages and within cultural customs of its day.

Scripture is brimming with customs, culture, and nature. Laying down my modern lenses gave me space to appreciate the beauty, embrace the difficulties, and let the stories pose their own questions. It's no surprise that I especially love the stories with animals who either play supporting characters, like the ravens that fed Elijah, or feature in a major role, such as the fish that swallowed Jonah.

Flash, lifting his head from the wildflowers, sucked in air and let out a booming *hee-HAW, hee-HAW, hee-HAW-HAW*. I smiled at the outlandish sound emanating from him. It reverberated around the field and seemed to bounce off the trees along the fence. His bray immediately brought to mind one of my favorite Bible stories, starring a talking donkey and a man named Balaam.

I never get tired of reading this head-scratching incident from the Israelites' journey to the Promised Land, but I used to get stuck on the logistics of the whole thing. *How, exactly, does a donkey talk?* You can find the account in Numbers 22, but I'll give you the Rachel Notes version here:

Balak, king of Moab, was terrified. The Israelites had already destroyed his Amorite neighbors on their march to the Promised Land, and now his own kingdom was in their path. King Balak persuasively hired Balaam, a renowned pagan seer, to take care of the problem by cursing God's chosen people.

So Balaam set out on his donkey to Moab, accompanied by two servants and the king's messengers, even though God had told Balaam not to go. Suddenly

Balaam's donkey bolted off the road and ran into a field.

What is going on? Balaam thought. He angrily beat his donkey (I'm not keen on that reaction!), then resumed the journey.

As the road narrowed between two vineyard walls, the donkey abruptly swerved and slammed Balaam's foot against the wall. Once again, the seer beat his donkey.

A few minutes later, without warning, the donkey stopped dead in her tracks and lay down, with Balaam still on her back.

"I've had enough of this!" Balaam rolled off the animal and took out his fury a third time.

He struck her repeatedly, and when Balaam raised his arm to hit her again, the donkey spoke: "Why are you beating me?"

"You've made me look like a fool!" Balaam shouted.

"I've been your donkey since the day you learned to ride," the donkey replied. "Have I ever behaved like this before?"

"No," Balaam admitted.

As soon as he answered, the Lord, who had given the donkey the ability to speak, opened Balaam's eyes. There, in the middle of the road, he saw the angel of the Lord holding a drawn sword. No wonder the donkey was frightened! And Balaam? Well, he was so scared that he fell facedown on the ground.

"Why did you beat your donkey?" the angel demanded. "I intentionally blocked the road because you knowingly disobeyed me. If the donkey hadn't seen me and reacted I would have killed you on the spot and spared the donkey."

What a dramatic divine intervention! I can imagine the Israelites retelling this story from their history numerous times, a requested favorite of the shepherds' children. A donkey who speaks their language! An angel gripping a sword! Eyes wide, they listen and learn.

They learn about a God who is actively involved in the world and how even the most talented "seers" can miss Him. They learn that a donkey, one of the lowliest animals on earth, can be given the gift of seeing with spiritual eyes and speaking in supernatural ways. It's a story of wonder, told with a touch of humor. (*A talking donkey? C'mon!*)

And yet, if God can use a donkey, He can surely use me, right? I nearly missed that lesson so many times in my rush to get through the story before too many questions came up. Now I was learning to slow down and sit with the message, to not be afraid of lingering awhile.

Flash brayed once again, and from my vantage point on the stump, he looked small and awfully alone by himself in the big field. Though his call made me smile, I quickly realized it was a plaintive plea to a friend, a message sent on the breeze to search for an answering whinny. His ears moved this way and that as he listened, hopeful for a distant response.

The joy and sadness and wistfulness in Flash's bray went straight to my soul. So much had happened in the last few months. Perhaps God was giving him the gift of speaking to me, just as he had done for Balaam's donkey. *Don't miss this! There's something spiritual happening here.*

I could relate to Flash's feelings. My joy in reading Scripture through new lenses was tinged with a bit of sadness in letting go of what I had done for years. Finding nuance and poetry and, yes, even humor in the Bible meant leaving behind a kind of comfortable fundamentalism and the certainty that came with it. In my need to grip every word tightly, I'd nearly missed the gorgeous Kingdom life that was trying to escape the boundaries of ink and paper to resuscitate my soul. Like Flash, I would have to trust the One in whose pasture I belonged, the One who would care for me, meet my needs, and lead me forward.

I stood and dusted off my jeans, and Flash saw my movement and turned to face me. The stump's rough surface had left a temporary indentation on the back of my thigh that pinched a nerve, and I hobbled toward him through the grass. He greeted me with a soft *phhhh* through his nostrils. I rubbed his neck, then made my way down the stripe on his back to the spot just above his tail. I pushed my fingertips through his thick coat, down to his skin, the way I knew he liked it best. Flash relaxed his back foot, clearly relishing the feeling of being touched by human hands once again.

God builds His Kingdom in such unexpected ways. He uses whatever means is available to Him: pastures, fishermen, widows, foreigners, outcasts, birds—even donkeys.

If God can use a donkey, He can surely use me.

God's presence everywhere means that nothing is beyond the scope of His power. Martin Luther observed that "God must be present in every single creature in its innermost and outermost being, on all sides, through and through, below and above, before and behind, so that nothing can be more truly present and within all creatures than God and God's power."

I resonate with Luther's words and personally believe the Reformer had a soft spot for all of God's creatures. In his lectures on Genesis, Luther said that "animals are designated as footprints of God."

It's up to us to open our eyes to the ways God is present and the means through which He speaks. Maybe it will be through a donkey! Maybe it will be through spending time in His creation. Maybe it will be through the heartfelt advice we don't want to consider from a friend. Maybe it will be through His living, breathing Scripture—when we don't rush through it but pay attention to its message.

What matters is that we don't miss the moment just because we're certain "it's not how He does it." God just might surprise us.

I left Flash and made my way back to the freshly mowed paths that circled and meandered through the field. Flash was still enjoying his newfound freedom, once again grazing in the last of the yellow wildflowers.

It's okay, buddy. I'll walk alone today.

"Come," the psalmist invites us.

Venite.

CHAPTER 8

Lead Us Not

Our Father, who art in heaven,
hallowed be thy Name,
thy kingdom come,
thy will be done,
on earth as it is in heaven.
Give us this day our daily bread.
And forgive us our trespasses,
as we forgive those who trespass against us.
And lead us not into temptation,
but deliver us from evil.
For thine is the kingdom,
and the power, and the glory,
for ever and ever. Amen.

"The Lord's Prayer," *The Book of Common Prayer*

"Is he ever going to learn how to walk forward?" Tom asked as I crouched down and called Henry to come.

"*Shh*. Leave him alone. He has issues." I kept my eyes on Henry as I slowly opened my hand to reveal a small carrot.

"Come! Come, Henry!" I called to him.

Henry had been resting just outside the barn, absorbing the morning sunshine, and now he looked at me with interest. The tall Texas bluestem grass hid his portly belly, and he swallowed another mouthful while considering my offer. Henry gazed at the carrot, glanced to see if Flash was in sight (he wasn't), and stepped toward me.

"See, he's getting better," I said brightly.

Ten feet out, Henry stopped.

"Here we go again," Tom said, leaning against the barn wall to watch the show.

With short crossover steps, Henry slowly pivoted 180 degrees. Then he stretched out his back foot and began inching his way toward me, *backward*. One slow step at a time.

"*Beep, beep, beep!*" Tom imitated a service vehicle's backup warning sound.

When Henry halted, his rump nearly ended up in my lap. I leaned to the right so I could see around him. He looked back at me with an expression of helpless embarrassment, as if his backside had taken on a mind of its own and insisted on being first.

"It's okay, Henderson. I understand." I reached up to scratch the top of his bum, then started to work my way up the dark stripe along his back. Henry let out his breath. Although his head was turned away, his ears were keenly listening to my voice.

"You're going to have to turn around if you want this carrot." I held it out to the side so he could see I still had it. He glanced over his shoulder and thought for several moments.

When you've been deeply hurt in the past, you can't be too careful.

Finally, he turned his body around and gingerly pulled the carrot into his mouth with his lips. He crunched on it, blinking slowly. My knee was killing me from crouching for so long, so I tried to adjust my position without startling him. Although Henry had no problem asserting himself with Flash, he was still shy around people. I couldn't imagine him ever walking in a parade like Doc Darlin had said, but then again, Doc *is* a donkey whisperer.

"Face it. Your donkey is weird." Tom winked at me as he left for the house.

As much as I had hoped Henry would wake up one morning and step in a new direction, he continued to approach me in reverse; it didn't seem to matter what the situation was. I gave up believing he would ever trust me enough to meet me head-on. He would always opt for the defensive posture that's instinctive to a small animal who might need to make a quick getaway.

But backing in is better than running away. Henry always came when I called; at least he trusted me enough to do that.

Maybe today will be the day . . .

I rubbed his dark, fuzzy ears and held out an apple slice. He investigated it with a sniff, then gave me a look: *What happened to the carrots?*

"I'm all out of carrots, Henry. I gave you the last one." I tried a positive parenting tactic that sometimes worked with my kids: "You get to try a new treat today! Yum!" I gave him a happy, excited smile.

Henry moved his lips halfheartedly, just enough to grasp the end of the apple slice. And there it hung, dangling halfway out of his mouth like a cigarette, his expression saying it all: *Yuck.*

He let his lower lip sag to dispatch the apple, but it was stuck, accentuating his pout.

"Really? You don't like apples? Who's ever heard of a donkey that doesn't like apples?" Henry didn't answer. He just gave me a dead stare as gravity slowly got the better of the apple wedge and it fell to the ground. He couldn't even bring himself to look at it.

Flash, seizing the opportunity, ambled over to the "disgusting" morsel on the ground and scarfed it down—*thankyouverymuch.*

Our training lesson was done for the day, so I reached for a curry brush. A recent rain had transformed the donkeys' favorite rolling spots into mud spas, and both had dried clods clinging to their hair. Flash's long mane looked like dreadlocks adorned with decorative beads.

"You first, buddy." Since they were still working out their hierarchy, I tried to attend to Flash before Henry when I could. It was important for Flash to know I considered him the leader. In donkey *theory*, it would help both of them relax in their roles rather than encourage competition. In donkey *reality*, it didn't seem to make a speck of difference.

I attempted to begin with Flash's mane, but he turned

around and insisted I start with his tail. He knew what he was doing. His tail is quite long, much like a horse's tail, and the dirt "beads" would take some time to brush out. He wouldn't mind the extra attention. Flash gave Henry a haughty, *See, I* AM *first* snort and then adjusted his posture for maximum relaxation.

There is something therapeutic about the grooming process. Working a curry brush over an appreciative donkey gives you a chance to let your mind rest. In a world filled with distractions and loud voices, the rhythmic sound of a brush comforts me. I enjoy watching the donkeys' reactions—exhaling contentedly and gently shaking their long ears. In these moments, all is right with the world. Worries lessen with every stroke, and anxious thoughts are dispelled with each burr and mud pellet that falls to the ground.

Our Father, who art in heaven,
hallowed be thy Name . . .

Henry backed in close, eager for his turn under the brush. Now I had two donkey backsides facing me, edging each other out. I scratched Henry's rump with one hand and continued brushing Flash. Hey, I can *try* to multitask, right? Henry stopped pushing back and finally let his ears settle to the sides of his head. *This is good enough for now.*

Thy kingdom come, thy will be done . . .

Maybe for some people, this wouldn't be the most inspirational setting for the Lord's Prayer, but something about it—maybe the earthiness of it all—seemed quite perfect for me. As I groomed and prayed the familiar words, saints who had gone before came to mind—especially my grandpa.

Grandpa Raaum was a Lutheran minister for forty-two years. I loved visiting him and my grandma at the prairie-style parsonage in their small Nebraska town, especially in the summer. Across the lawn was the church with its tall steeple and bell, which Grandpa would ring on Sunday mornings to announce service times.

Grandpa was old-school. He made weekly rounds— mostly on foot—to visit parishioners who were sick, stopping at their homes within the town's ten square blocks. Each Saturday night, he mimeographed the weekly church bulletins in his home office, the smell of ink filling the entire house while we kids watched the papers land one by one in a damp stack.

On Sundays, Grandpa wore clerical robes (he told me they were called vestments), a white one over a black one, along with a collar and a stole—a long, wide silk band that hung around his neck and past his knees. The colors changed according to the liturgical season on the church calendar.

These church-related terms were foreign to me but were interesting nonetheless. My parents, commissioned as young Lutheran missionaries to Mexico, had seen the transformational power and gifts of the Holy Spirit within the charismatic movement of the late 1960s, and they embraced them completely. It meant breaking with their mission board, but it set them on an exciting path that allowed more freedom to follow God's leading.

During my elementary and middle school years, we moved from Mexico to the Pacific Northwest, where my dad served an independent charismatic church. Our services were much more free-flowing and exuberant than those I experienced at Grandpa's church. I loved the praise choruses and informality that were hallmarks of our worship. Why would anyone prefer a more traditional style that seemed so stiff and scripted?

And yet, when I was inside Grandpa's church, there was something that gripped me. Its wood floor and pews, the stained glass windows and baptismal font—even the basement where Vacation Bible Schools (and potlucks and wedding/anniversary/funeral receptions) took place—well, they felt . . . I didn't know how to describe it then. Now I know the word I was looking for: *sacred*.

The sanctuary was so different from the school gymnasium where our church met. The atmosphere of the gym was casual and welcoming, and we kids could noisily release our energy by playing Four Square or shooting baskets while the adults set up folding chairs for the service. When I stepped into Grandpa's church, everything was hushed and ceremonial. It was like entering another country—one with a different language and culture than my own. Each service left me wishing for more, even though I considered it outdated.

Dinner at my grandparents' house took place at the dining room table—the kitchen table was for breakfast and lunch. My mom carried on that tradition in our family too. Grandma would never use paper plates, no matter how simple the meal. In the summer, we always had plenty of vegetables from the garden—sweet corn, beets, carrots, and peas—served with

Swedish meatballs or stewed chicken. We kids would finish eating long before the adults and get antsy waiting to be excused.

Our clean plates cued Grandpa to open his well-worn Bible. He would clear his throat and begin. "In Jesus' name," he would say, then pause momentarily before continuing.

We were already familiar with postdinner devotions. Usually my dad read from a Bible storybook, and we would look over his shoulder at the pictures.

Grandpa's Scripture reading felt sooo long, especially without the benefit of pictures. Looking back, it was probably only one short psalm, but it seemed to go on forever. When he finished, he'd bow his head. "Let us pray."

We'd all join in.

"Our Father, who art in heaven, hallowed be thy Name . . ."

As soon as my siblings and I heard the *Amen*, we jumped to our feet, picked up our plates, and carried them to the kitchen sink. After the *entire* table had been cleared, we were free for the night. We could go to the local pool for an evening swim or play a rousing game of badminton in the yard until it was too dark to see the shuttlecock.

When I was reciting the Lord's Prayer during those childhood visits, it seemed repetitious and superfluous. *Every night after dinner? Seems a bit much.*

Yes, these were Jesus' words, what He taught His disciples to pray—a pretty good prayer "example." As an adult, I have heard some suggest the Lord's Prayer might help "prime the pump" for deeper heartfelt prayers that can arm you for spiritual warfare or provide a more meaningful worship experience. Like a writing prompt ("Write about your first day of kindergarten— GO!"), the Lord's Prayer—with its simple framework—could serve to inspire personal prayers. But did it really need to be said daily as a stand-alone offering? Perhaps once a month would do.

Oh, Grandpa, your old-fashioned ways are so quaint.

Or so I thought.

I gave up trying to help Henry come to me "properly." His unconventional approach didn't hurt anyone and only endeared him to me all the more.

One afternoon as I was in the barn arranging some boxes of out-of-season clothing I wanted to store, I saw Flash and Henry emerge from the backwoods. Flash caught sight of me and picked up his pace, with Henry following behind—moving *forward*. I pointed to the hay I'd set out to keep them occupied while I did my work, and Flash quickly veered off to begin snacking.

I looked at Henry. At the point I expected him to halt and put it into reverse, he held my gaze—and just kept coming.

"Oh, Henry," I whispered in encouragement. "Look at you, darling boy." He was coming headfirst, ears up and striped legs striding confidently, straight to me. He came to a stop and sniffed my hand.

I knelt down, took his face in my hands, and kissed his little nose.

"You did it, Henderson Number Ten. You did it."

Now, I know you probably think I cry a lot, but you've got to admit this was a perfectly acceptable moment for me to wipe some tears away. Henry didn't seem to mind. He snuggled in closer as if he had known how big his breakthrough was.

Waiting for Henry to trust me enough to meet me face-forward took patience and understanding. It couldn't be rushed. He had done it without fanfare, and the payoff was undeniably sweet.

I savored the victory and wasn't even going to *think* about training him to walk with me on a lead until he proved he was making consistent "headway."

One thing at a time.

∧ ∧

"I can't believe we are able to talk about this in church," Tom whispered as he leaned toward me. We'd happened upon a science and faith series at a Methodist church in Dallas and jumped at the chance to attend. Tom had become discouraged in his quest to discuss his questions about the topic with our own church staff and others in our circle of friends and family. Most had little interest in or knowledge about the questions on his mind, and several shared a concern that asking about the age of the universe could quickly lead down the slippery slope that ends in atheism.

Now we found ourselves in a roomful of people on a Sunday morning, listening to a serious discussion on this topic that was so important to us. "Even if our generation doesn't care, our kids and grandkids certainly will," Tom said. My mind nearly exploded with joy at the freedom to explore the immensity and complexity of creation and discover what it tells us about our amazing God.

The class began at 11:00 a.m., but we had decided to attend the church service beforehand, just to see what it was like. As a member of nondenominational Bible churches for more than thirty years, I'd never been to a Methodist service and had very little idea what to expect.

I take that back—I did have expectations.

I'm embarrassed to say I expected to hear a watered-down

gospel message, experience a social-club atmosphere, and be unimpressed by shallow spirituality. I expected to be under-whelmed by the hymn singing (sorry, Wesley brothers). I expected it to be dry. Memories of Grandpa's services came to mind. Perhaps it was never overtly stated in my circles, but in so many ways they had implied that denominational churches were dead.

This is what I perceived all mainline churches to be like:

Mainline church = lifeless.

Evangelical church = alive.

Mainline = social gospel.

Evangelical = true gospel.

Those perceptions were shattered at that 9:30 a.m. service.

I walked into the ninety-year-old sanctuary and looked up at the massive wooden arches and soaring ceiling. The center aisle, flanked by rows of pews, led my eyes to the pulpit standing in front, the robed choir sitting in the loft, and the magnificent organ pipes filling the front walls of the church. Immediately, a lump formed in my throat. The room felt so different from the all-purpose sanctuary/gymnasium of the church Tom and I attended and the other modern church auditoriums where we normally felt comfortable.

I was in another country.

Sacred, I thought. *This feels sacred.*

Stained glass windows. Did I mention the stained glass?

I felt as if I'd come home.

During the service, the congregation stood to say the Apostles' Creed, which was printed in the bulletin so visitors like Tom and me could join in. I'd already committed it to memory and had been making it part of my regular prayer walks, but saying it out loud with a congregation was far different than reciting it by myself. I was so moved that I couldn't make it through the entire Creed.

Next, we sang a hymn, heard a gospel reading from Matthew, and prayed the Lord's Prayer together. Again, the words were right there in the bulletin but blurred by my tears. Behind us, a small boy's voice mingled with the voices of the elderly couple next to us as we prayed in unison. Somewhere in there, Tom's voice stopped. Out of the corner of my eye, I could see he was wiping his eyes too.

As I sat down with the rest of the congregation, I wondered, *Did I make it a point to teach the Lord's Prayer to my children as they were growing up? Did they experience it as a regular part of worship?* Maybe they'd learned it, but I didn't recall it being a priority, either at home or at church.

The remainder of the service—a clear gospel sermon and the closing benediction, sung together—was equally impactful.

Where had *this* been all my life?

Perhaps Grandpa Raaum had known something, in his "quaint" Lutheran ways, that I'd somehow missed. There was a loveliness in traditions like these, a sweetness and a sacredness that felt transcendent.

We had come for the science/faith discussion and left with the realization that we'd become smug and myopic in our faith stream. Here were brothers and sisters in Christ, devoted followers of Jesus, whom I had looked at askance. *These poor people don't know what they're missing. Surely they aren't as "on fire" as we are. Surely their recitations of the Lord's Prayer are just "vain repetitions."*

Something like shame stole over me. No, actually it *was*

shame. My disdain for liturgical worship was rooted in a sense of superiority, and I hated to admit it. In our desire to experience freedom of expression, we evangelicals have created a whole new kind of liturgy—a standard way of worship with an emphasis on "new, relevant, and exciting." Our goal is to avoid a ho-hum religion, and if that means featuring lights and smoke, elaborate stage sets, a full band, and multimedia presentations . . . bring 'em on. This kind of worship service can certainly be meaningful and help us feel closer to God, so I'm not knocking it. I understand the motivation to engage our contemporary sensibilities, and I've been part of worship teams who crafted such experiences with deep sincerity.

But a level of impoverishment I didn't know I had emerged in that Methodist service. It reminded me of stories my grandma had told me about getting oranges in her Christmas stockings as a child. When I asked her if she felt sad about receiving such meager gifts, she laughed. "We didn't know any different! We thought everybody only got oranges in their stockings." She didn't know her family was poor until she was old enough to go to school and learned that other children received toys and new clothes as Christmas gifts. Suddenly her oranges no longer seemed extravagant.

That morning in church I encountered riches—spiritual riches—and I wanted them for myself. Corporately praying the Lord's Prayer as an integral part of worship was like discovering a gold mine. It linked me with millions upon millions of faithful Christians around the world who were *also* praying the Lord's Prayer and affirming the Creeds together in solidarity and obedience to Jesus. I was humbled to be among them.

When we left the church that day, I was inspired to begin praying the Lord's Prayer daily. It wasn't a formal commitment but merely a trial run. Even though I knew the words by heart, I copied them into my notebook because I wanted the prayer to have a place of importance in my growing collection. Seeing the words in my own unadorned handwriting seemed to help me absorb them.

Morning and evening, I paused on each phrase, letting the words sink in and do their work in my mind and heart. It seemed like any occasion presented a perfect opportunity—as I drove the car, washed dishes, walked in the pasture, or waited to fall asleep at night.

Jesus said to his disciples, "When you pray, say *this* . . ." Until now I had taken those words as a mere suggestion, a guideline for more important prayers. Now I began to take them as a clear directive.

I bought a couple of books that unpacked the Lord's Prayer even more and took one writer's words especially to heart:

Maybe you can't even remember the last time you said it. And yet, the saying of the Lord's Prayer is one of the most explicit instructions that Jesus gives us in the New Testament. It is one of the simplest ways that we can practice being a follower of his.

Thy kingdom come, thy will be done . . .

It's hard to pray those words from the heart without being changed.

^ ^

Henry continued as a work in progress. Sometimes he came to me headfirst; other times he stopped and rotated like a train engine on a turntable and backed up his caboose. I could never predict which end I'd see first.

Despite my earlier decision to wait, I decided it was time to work with him on a lead. Up until now, I had always led Flash (still giving him the leadership role) and let Henry follow along after us without a halter or rope.

Putting a halter on Henry? A piece of cake. He stuck his nose into the apparatus like a true professional and even let me buckle it. Getting him to follow me on a lead rope? Yeah, not so much.

For our first lesson, I stood near the left side of Henry's head, pulled the lead a little with my right hand, and spoke a gentle command: "Walk on! Walk on, Henry!"

The second lesson is, obviously, the meaning of "Whoa." Of course, you have to be *moving* in order to get to "Whoa." Henry wasn't there. His tail was moving, but his feet were planted firmly in place.

"Walk on, Henry!" I repeated with another small tug.

Okay. You can decide on your own. I let the lead go slack and made sure he knew I had a treat for him.

Henry decided not to respond.

"Walk on! Come on!" I again let him know my wishes with the lead rope and a treat. *Sweet feed, don't fail me now.*

This time, Henry moved.

In a circle.

He turned himself around and began to walk _____.

You can fill in the blank . . .

Yes, backward.

"Henry, seriously? You can't go on a walk with me like this!"

He didn't care. He had to do it his way.

My walks with Henry turned into pasture "waits." When it was time to venture off, Henry had to stretch a back foot behind him, feel for the ground, step his front legs back, and then do the same with his other back foot.

Backward step by backward step, he was making progress, and I had to give him credit. Moving this way, he couldn't see what was up ahead, yet he trusted me enough to keep going. I came across a quote from Oswald Chambers that resonated in some ways with what was happening with Henry, and it definitely applied to my own spiritual journey as well: "Faith never knows where it is being led, but it loves and knows the One Who is leading."

Waiting for Henry each day gave me time to think. The summerlong series at the Methodist church made Tom and me realize it was time to move on and embrace another way of walking out our faith. I hadn't realized how small my personal practice of faith had become or how difficult it would be to leave my tribe. It was made of good people who were fine Christians, and I loved them. Would I be judged for leaving our church? Considered a backslider?

I'd been longing for a deeper sense of the sacred, one rich with ritual and tradition, and for a faith home that wouldn't look sideways at our questions. This Methodist church seemed a perfect fit—it possessed a deep love for Jesus, an intense devotion to Scripture, beautiful liturgical worship, and an openness to discuss (and differ on) "nonessential" matters like science and biblical interpretations.

We had prayed the Lord's Prayer every Sunday. Out loud. All together. It did something to me, although I can't explain it. Perhaps it was part of the mystery I'd been longing for.

In many ways, I was just like Henry. I wanted to go where God was leading me, but I was nervous to see where that path might go. Scared of change. Afraid to follow. Backing into God's leading is one way to get there, but it's not the most efficient or most enjoyable. You see where you've already been, not where you need to go.

"Lead me."

I stopped on that line. I was praying the Lord's Prayer with Henry in tow, still in reverse gear.

Lead me to green pastures.

Lead me to success.

Lead me to the right job.

Lead me to new opportunities.

Henry had stopped too, and he appeared to be thinking.

"You can do it, Henry. Turn your chubster self around," I encouraged him.

Henry ignored my advice by sticking out a back foot and continuing on. I rolled my eyes, but what could I say? He was moving, and for now that was enough.

Lead me to higher ground.

Lead me to security.

Lead me to the right church.

While you're at it, lead me to a good bargain at Target, Lord.

I wondered why the Lord told us to pray, "Lead us not into

temptation." Who would ever think He would lead us *there*? James certainly didn't, writing in his epistle, "And remember, when you are being tempted, do not say, 'God is tempting me.' God is never tempted to do wrong, and he never tempts anyone else" (James 1:13).

Flash came from behind the barn to check on Henry and me, giving us a *phhhh* as he sauntered by. Henry laid his ears back and nipped at Flash's legs.

"Ignore him, Henderson. You can take all the time you need, and don't feel bad about it." I patted his rump and watched a tiny dust cloud form and blow away. He threw me a look of relief over his shoulder.

Hey, no judgment here, bud.

I adjusted the rope and gave him a little more slack. As I made my way down the path, followed by a small donkey walking backward, I thought, *Well, aren't we a ridiculous sight? And yet our slow pace gave me more time to think.*

Perhaps Jesus knew that if He had given us words like "Lead us in Your will," we'd find ways of imagining our own desires as His will. As it is, I do enough demanding and requesting in my prayers. Maybe Jesus knew that the very things we ask to be led to are the very things that will tempt us most.

Green pastures are wonderful, but they may tempt me to feel full, lethargic, and lazy.

Success may be the answer to my prayer but might also bring opportunity for pride.

The "perfect job" may be just what I was hoping for, but it could also lead me to become self-sufficient.

The "right" church may fill a spiritual need, but I might be tempted to look back and criticize my past faith journey rather than accept it with gratefulness.

Ouch. The fact was, as I learned new ways of praying, reading Scripture, and experiencing worship, I kept asking myself, *How could I have missed this? Why did no one ever tell me about these different faith practices?* I'd spent my entire life in churches and immersed in the Bible, yet I had spent so little time getting to know Jesus beyond His mission to die for my sins. I'd not taken His teaching as anything more serious than simply a *preamble* to the Big Moment on the cross, and I hadn't even bothered to pray as He had prayed.

I was moving on but looking backward, just like Henry.

Lead us . . . but lead us not into temptation.

Jesus does indeed lead us and guide us, and He knows our frailties and tendencies. He gives us a gentle tug to say, "This way! You can do it!" and then waits for us to come along as we feel our way backward with our feet rather than turning to face into His good plan. Looking back means we can't sense the blessings that may lie ahead. Holding on to what's familiar feels like the safest thing to do, but it prevents us from growing.

Following God is a sacred journey. With each step, we participate in God's Kingdom "on earth, as it is in heaven." The apostle Paul said it in the beginning of his sermon at Mars Hill in Athens: "He made from one man every nation . . . that they should seek God, and perhaps feel their way toward him and find him. Yet he is actually not far from each one of us."

Henry turned his head around to look at me, his ears wiggling in question.

"You can do it, Henry. You've got this," I encouraged him

one more time. He swished his tiny tail and then . . . began to pivot. I caught my breath. "That's the way!"

Three more steps and he was facing forward—finally. I bent down and kissed him on his soft nose. His expression said it all: *I trust you.*

"Walk on, Henry," I whispered. "Walk on."

CHAPTER 9

Infected Hearts

O God, you made us in your own image
and redeemed us through Jesus your Son:
Look with compassion on the whole human family;
take away the arrogance and hatred
which infect our hearts;
break down the walls that separate us;
unite us in bonds of love;
and work through our struggle and confusion
to accomplish your purposes on earth;
that, in your good time, all nations
and races may serve you
in harmony around your heavenly throne;
through Jesus Christ our Lord. Amen.

Prayers for the World: "For the Human Family,"
The Book of Common Prayer

was dusting off the bookshelves in Grayson's old room when I found them.

The bottom shelves still housed his favorite books: *My Side of the Mountain*, *Hatchet*, *The Call of the Wild*, and of course, *Calvin and Hobbes*. The upper shelves displayed a few model train engines and cars, along with various trophies, ribbons, and hockey pucks. In the corner was "Buddy," his boyhood nighttime rag doll.

As I propped Buddy up, I noticed a pair of 3-D movie glasses stuck behind the books—a souvenir from *Toy Story 3*. I held them in my hands and was transported back in time, when the whole world seemed to be going nuts over using the technology in this Disney film. Everyone was hyping the movie.

"Breathtaking!"

"Magical!"

"Vivid!"

"Amazing!"

"Astounding!"

Tom and I took Grayson, then in high school but still a Woody and Buzz Lightyear fan, and eagerly shelled out the extra money for the 3-D experience ("So worth it!"). We bought a tub of popcorn to share, found our seats, tore open the packages containing our special glasses, and waited for the movie to begin. Suddenly I realized I needed to visit the ladies' room on account of, well . . . three birthed babies, time, and let's just say "gravity." I glanced at my watch. *Just enough time before the movie starts.*

When I returned, I had only missed a minute. I sat back and got comfortable, reached in my purse for my special glasses, and looked at the screen.

Wait a second. Wait just a blasted second.

The colors were muddy.

The picture was blurry.

The animation was grainy.

Everything was dark.

In short, it was absolutely terrible!

Stop the movie; we've all been had!

I looked around the theater and then at Tom and Grayson. Everyone was pretending to enjoy it—smiling, laughing, and gobbling handfuls of popcorn.

Uh-uh. You can't fool me. You overhype a movie, convince people to pay more, and then no one says anything about the horrid quality because they're too embarrassed to be the "only one" disappointed in it?

Remember *The Emperor's New Clothes*? Like the child in the fable, I, and I alone, would be the one person with an ounce of courage to challenge this farce! Just as I was about to stand up and shout the truth to the audience, Tom turned and looked at me with an excited smile on his face.

Then . . . his smile faded to a quizzical look, one eyebrow up.

"Rachel, why are you wearing your sunglasses?"

What? My hand flew to my face to grab the tinted glasses.

Well, that certainly explained things. I quickly found the correct lenses and put them on.

OH MY.

The movie was breathtaking!

The lifelike effects were magical!

The colors were so vivid they popped!

The animation was truly amazing!

I was astounded by the brilliance.

Okay, now I get it!

3-D technology was truly marvelous.

The thing is, the movie hadn't changed. The projectionist hadn't switched reels when I was fumbling for my glasses.

The only thing that had changed from moments before was my glasses.

The right lenses made all the difference.

∧ ∧

I hoisted the fifty-pound salt block from the back of the Suburban and immediately lost my grip. It thudded to the ground, just missing my toes. *How does Bill lift these things so easily?* I somehow managed to carry the mineral-laced cube most of the way to its usual spot under the cedar trees—until I gave up and rolled it the final ten feet.

Henry was first to emerge from behind the barn to see what the commotion was about. I didn't realize I'd been grunting with each flip-and-shove movement of the block, and now he peered at me with a mixture of pity, thanks, and amusement.

Henry. With his ears perked forward and his liquid brown eyes looking straight into mine, I couldn't help but engage him in baby talk. "Hi, Henwy! Hi, cutie-pie!" I reached out a hand to beckon him to come to Mama. As he took a step toward me, I thought we might have a moment of bonding affection, but instead Flash came thundering around the corner and bumped Henry off course.

Back to reality.

Ears back, Henry nipped at Flash's neck, telling him, "Me first, pal." Flash responded by coming in hot and hip-checking Henry into the fence.

"Guys, guys! Give it a rest, will ya?"

The donkeys quit their jockeying for line leader long enough to give me identical looks that could only be translated, *I will if he will.*

I sighed. Henry had been here for months, and I'd done my best to follow Doc Darlin's advice to wait for a real friendship to develop. At best, Flash and Henry had a "relationship"—a general understanding of each other's boundaries—but still not an emotional attachment. I certainly didn't see any signs of it yet.

It was clear that Flash considered Henry an interruption in his well-ordered life. He'd had his schedule, his routine, his *life* that he'd pieced back together after Penny. He had survived alone and was content. Then along came this little scrapper with an oversized attitude that shook up Flash's existence. As completely adorable as Henry was, he came with baggage—the need to be loved and the desire to be the boss. Neither of those traits had gone over well with Flash, who was not about to relinquish his title as Supreme Leader of the Pasture without a fight.

"Flash, if you can just learn to love him, Henry will relax and stop trying to take your position." My reasoning seemed to fall on deaf ears.

Henry, still steaming from the hip-check, insisted that he get first dibs at the salt block. While Henry licked s . . . l . . . o . . . w . . . l . . . y away as if there were no line behind him, I put my arm around Flash's neck. He nosed my shirt and nibbled at it with his rubbery lips before his tongue found the salt residue still clinging to the fabric.

Flash was a good donkey, and I loved him. "Thanks for giving Henry space," I told him.

A moment later, I took my comment back. Flash moved away from my warm embrace to shove Henry, then claimed the salt block as his own.

Flash, will you ever see Henry as anything but a threat to your peaceful existence? I shook my head and headed back to my studio to get some work done. I'd finished the project with Bridgette and was excited about a new art commission for an upscale retail space in north Dallas. My assignment was to create several original mixed-media pieces as part of a decorative redesign of the area, and I couldn't wait to get started.

An e-mail from our son-in-law Nathan greeted me on the computer.

"There is a single mom with three kids who is in between apartments and has no place to go. They need a place to stay for about a month, until she can get her feet underneath her and find a new living situation."

There was no pressure to act on the message; Nathan was simply casting a wide net to his circle of friends in case someone might be able to help. He and Meghan had gotten to know Shonda through a ministry they'd worked with and connected with her in a special way. They'd been part of her life for several years and were especially involved with the kids.

As much as I wish we could help, Nathan, this isn't an ideal time, I thought. *Certainly someone will step up.*

The truth was, Tom was immersed in his new business, and with my new project at hand, we were both feeling a bit overwhelmed. We felt the need to focus on getting ourselves into a steadier pace of life.

We prayed together for Shonda and her family and then began working through our to-do lists for the day. Tom passed me in the laundry room later. "With the kids gone, we do have two empty bedrooms," he mentioned casually.

"We do," I replied with a nod. "Only one of them has a bed in it, though." Grayson had needed his bed in his college apartment.

"Shonda works nights, so the kids really just need a place to crash," Tom said, recalling details from the e-mail.

"True."

"I think they should stay with us," we both concluded simultaneously. We could get air mattresses and sleeping bags to use as temporary beds.

Shonda and her three children—Morgan, fifteen; Devon, eleven; and Missy, ten—arrived with a couple of suitcases, school backpacks, and a few treasured items. Missy brought her prized possession—a Barbie Dreamhouse—and spent hours making decorations out of construction paper I had on hand, as well as making lists of furniture and accessories she wanted.

Shonda regularly juggled two or three part-time jobs to make ends meet and slept only a few hours a night. In the first week, we hardly even saw her, except if she happened to be catching up on sleep during daylight hours, and I peeked through the bedroom doorway to check on her.

She brought food for the kids to eat because she didn't want to inconvenience us, but I quickly realized it only made sense to buy extra groceries and share meals together. Ever since Grayson had gone off to college, I'd gotten lazy about cooking for just Tom and me. After almost thirty years, I was enjoying not planning meals and relished the luxury of picking up takeout whenever we wanted. Suddenly, here I was cooking for an additional four people, eating with the kids, and putting extra plates of food in the fridge for Shonda to take to work. The kitchen was filled with laughter and mouthwatering smells and a sink full of dishes.

It was all good.

"Morgan, could you go upstairs and make sure Missy and Devon brush their teeth and get ready for bed?" I asked one night. With Shonda gone in the evenings, I had to reach back into my memory and recall what it took to get kids in bed at a decent time. Later, I went in to say good night and make sure they were comfortable.

Unfortunately, it would take me more than two weeks to realize that many of the essentials I take for granted—pajamas, toothpaste, toothbrushes, basic toiletries—were luxury items our guests did not have.

The kids never let on.

They just went upstairs and pretended I hadn't asked them to fly to the moon and back before calling it a day. They even convinced me they liked sleeping in their clothes.

The clues were there, but I didn't see them. My heart broke when I realized how much I'd assumed.

Suddenly I found that I was seeing life through new lenses.

A scene from my teenage years in Mexico came to mind one evening as I made a pot of spaghetti for everyone.

I was in a taxi and had just told the driver where I wanted to go. His eyes met mine in the rearview mirror.

"Your eyes are blue!" he exclaimed. "Is that the real color of your eyes?"

"Yes, blue is my real eye color," I said.

"Does everything look blue?" he asked.

"Of course not!" I responded. "I see everything just the same as you do!"

"What color is that car?" The driver pointed to a white Volkswagen.

"Oh, that's blue," I teased him.

When he looked startled, I thought I'd better explain. "No, no, it's white. I was just kidding."

He wasn't convinced. After more minutes of discussion and going back and forth identifying various colors all around us, I finally managed to persuade him.

As I stirred the spaghetti sauce for six in my kitchen, it hit me. *That taxi driver may have been right all along.* His brown eyes and my blue eyes probably *did* see the world in very different ways. Sure, we both saw white Volkswagens, but my blue eyes, accompanied by my fair skin and blonde hair, had also seen a world full of possibilities. It had never occurred to me that blue eyes and blonde hair might have *created* some of those possibilities to begin with. In my view, hard work and determination would always make a way no matter the color of your eyes. After all, people are kind and good, and they will give you a fair chance, right?

Look with compassion
on the whole human family . . .

They didn't know it, but the African American family staying in our spare bedrooms was helping Tom and me begin to see a different world—one through their beautiful brown eyes. For the first time, I saw another reality I'd unknowingly dismissed. I guess because I felt I'd worked hard for everything I'd achieved and thought nothing had been handed to me, I had always insisted the "playing field is level." I'd bristled at the thought that someone might receive a scholarship—or a job opportunity or a helping hand—on the basis of race. Now, I wondered what good a level playing field even *was* if you could *never get on it* in the first place. I began to see the complexity of race and cultural bias and the challenges that come with poverty and lack.

Without a dependable car, Shonda relied on a friend to get her to and from work. She was able to use our computer to access e-mail and Internet, but under normal circumstances she would have to walk to a library—if one happened to be within walking distance. Shonda hoped that in the month they would live with us, she could save enough money to cover rent and utility deposits for a new apartment—preferably within a good school district. Her children had already been in three different districts in the past three years and needed some assistance catching up.

Up close and personal, I could see the ways poverty perpetuates itself—generation after generation. I saw my own complicity in blaming people for "bad choices" or "not working hard enough." *If I were living in the same circumstances, would I make better choices? Would I take on a second minimum wage job and try to get by on less sleep?*

I suddenly saw the privilege I was born into.

Opening our home to a homeless family was a huge interruption in our well-planned lives. It was the difference between "helping the poor" by putting money in the offering plate—or sending our monthly donation to a child in a third world country via autopay—and truly knowing a *specific* struggling family and their individual plight. There is nothing like living with others, day in and day out, to find out how little you really understand.

To say it was humbling would be an understatement.

Writer Neil Gaiman put his finger on it for me: "The gulf that exists between us as people is that when we look at each other we might see faces, skin color, gender, race, or attitudes, but we don't see, we can't see, the stories."

As much as I enjoy telling stories, I had not seen theirs.

∧ ∧

By the end of the month, Tom and I knew it was not enough to simply send this family on their way. A house across the street became available to rent, and we jumped on it. We crowdsourced money to help with rent and utility deposits, gathered donated furniture and household items, and found friends to help move them in. Tom and I continued to assist however we could. We knew it wouldn't be a permanent solution for the family, but we hoped we could help the kids make it through the school year while Shonda found stable employment.

One morning while I was eating breakfast, there was a knock on our door. I opened it to find Morgan standing there. "I missed the bus," she said apologetically.

She had fallen back asleep after Shonda had woken her before leaving for work. Morgan didn't have an alarm clock, and the younger kids had already left for school. This wasn't the first time it had happened, and to be honest, I felt inconvenienced to have to drive her to school again. Little things on her to-do list, like getting to school on time, or printing out homework assignments, or creating displays from craft supplies, reminded me how uncomplicated it had been for my children to accomplish those same kinds of tasks. The materials were already in the house, and if we ran out, our budget could handle a trip to the craft store for more construction paper and glue. We had time and resources for our kids, and their assignments were well done and professional looking. Their school careers set them up for success in ways I hadn't given a second thought to.

Our arrangement with Shonda and her family turned out to be both exhausting and wonderful, messy and beautiful. We were stretched in every way. I readily admit the road of love is hard. I had been far more possessive with my time and money than I ever believed I was. My heart was infected with selfishness. Tom and I both became acutely aware of how little we'd concerned ourselves with the needs of others, especially those who didn't look like us.

For the first time, we saw ourselves reflected in others around us who were initially very generous with money, food, and furnishings but then seemed to trickle away when the needs were ongoing and the recipients had "used up" their measure of goodwill. My phone calls to unsnarl bureaucratic red tape showed me how easily a family can slip through the cracks and continue to struggle when that assistance runs out. Was it a coincidence that the prayer "For the Human Family" had made its way into my heart?

O God, . . . break down the walls that
separate us; unite us in bonds of love . . .

∧ ∧

"Miss Rachel, I think the donkeys are killing each other!" Missy yelled from outside. She was eating her after-school snack at the table near the fence. I ran out to see Flash and Henry biting and kicking each other with an alarming ferocity. Henry grabbed Flash's neck with his teeth and brought him down with a thud.

"Henry! Let go! Let him go!" I yelled angrily. Why wouldn't he stop?

"He's hurting Flash!" Missy cried, visibly upset.

"Henderson! Henderson Number Ten!"

I clapped and hollered, and Henry finally let go, only to turn and buck, hitting Flash in the chin with his back feet. Flash hopped up from his knees and went for Henry's neck but missed. Henry was too small and agile. Flash was easily out-gunned by Henry, who deftly got in another bite before Flash even knew what was happening.

Why couldn't these two get along better? Their "play," something donkeys naturally do, inevitably turned sour, and they hurt each other unnecessarily. They bit too fiercely, kicked too hard. Rather than becoming friends, Flash and Henry seemed intent on jockeying for position and allowing their fear and rivalry to keep them apart.

When Flash was all alone in his pasture, he seemed perfectly content, mild mannered, and easily satisfied. Henry brought out Flash's less virtuous characteristics—jealousy, meanness, and privilege—that were there all along but never truly visible. Until now, Flash had never been put in a situation where he had to think about anyone but himself.

This is what interruptions do. At least, that's what they *should* do. They make us step back and take a second look, reassess, and adjust our glasses.

"Missy, I think these donkeys need a change of scenery," I said. "Would you like to help me take them for a walk?"

Missy looked at me as if I were crazy. "I don't want to get close to them! I'm scared."

"Oh, they were just playing," I told her. "See how they've calmed down now?" She looked at Henry, who was now staring at her through the fence, almost willing her to take him. "They've gotten the stink out of their britches now, and they'll be happy to just walk along with us."

"I don't know," Missy replied hesitantly while I reached for their halters that were hanging on a hook near the gate.

"It's okay if you just want to watch us," I reassured her. Missy looked relieved. Taking another bite of her cracker and cheese, she settled back in her chair, swinging her legs back and forth. She was cute as could be, and the more time I spent with Missy and her family, the more I worried about their future. What would they do if Shonda's job situation didn't improve?

Missy put her cracker down suddenly and pointed at Henry. "What's wrong with his legs?" she asked.

Henry's back legs were raw with bites and fresh blood. Horseflies were buzzing around him everywhere, and he stamped his foot to try and shake them off.

"He's being eaten up by flies!" I said, setting down the halters. "Missy, run inside and get some carrots, would you?" I needed to spray Henry down with the fly repellent we kept in the tack room. He had never been spritzed with a liquid before, and I didn't know how he would feel about the process.

Henry watched me return with the giant spray bottle, his eyes wary. I set it down behind me, took the carrots from Missy, and sweet-talked him into letting me put on his halter and lead rope. I could tell he knew something was up.

"It's okay, buddy," I tried to reassure him. "Here's a carrot for you. You munch on that while we take care of these flies." As soon as I squeezed the trigger, Henry jerked back and tried to run away. I hung on to the rope and swung him back around toward me, barely maintaining my balance. Another quick spray, and this time he reared, front feet up, his white belly toward me. Now he was panicked and leaned back hard, trying to escape. He pulled me around in circles, unwilling to stand still for one second.

This isn't going to work without Tom's help. Setting the fly spray as far away from him as I could, I let Henry see I didn't have it anymore and continued to try and calm him. He stamped his back foot and swished his tail, the flies clearly irritating him. *If you'd only stand still long enough for me to get a couple of sprays in!* He had no idea I was trying to help him. I removed his rope and turned to Flash, who, along with Missy, had been watching the whole event.

Of course!

"Flash, you want to show him how it's done? I should have started with you so he could see it's nothing to be afraid of." I brought the bottle over and proceeded to generously spray his legs (which showed little sign of the flies) as well as his entire body. He stood quietly and seemed, in fact, to enjoy it! I glanced at Henry, who clearly was not buying this charade after being so traumatized. He was convinced the spray was evil and stayed beyond my reach, just to be on the safe side. He would have to suffer a little longer until I could either rub the repellent on him or get Tom's help to spray him.

"Let's get this walk going," I said, clipping Flash's lead on. When Flash and Henry weren't bugging each other, they were lovely to be around. I knew if I started leading Flash, Henry would probably follow along at his own pace. Since we would stay inside the fence, I wouldn't even need to put a lead on him.

The vast, blue Texas sky enticed me to look up, bidding me to step away and decompress from my anxieties over Shonda and her precious family. God understood that I was out of words. He was quite content to walk with me in silence, and so was Flash. Donkeys never chatter unnecessarily. Yes, Flash needed some convincing to follow along on the lead rope, but even the silent exchange of opinions was a welcome change of pace:

You're coming with me.

I don't want to come.

You're coming.

No.

Yes!

Okay . . .

Once I'd pressed Flash into going along, he walked as willingly as if it had been his idea in the first place. Henry lingered near Missy for another minute before following at a distance. For whatever reason, he wouldn't let Flash out of his sight, even if *I* wasn't his favorite person just then.

Deep breath. Be in the moment, Rachel. Let your mind settle. One of Jesus' stories began to fill my mind while the three of us walked. I always pictured Jesus outside, surrounded by people who leaned in close to hear what He had to say.

One day an expert in religious law stood up to test Jesus by asking him this question: "Teacher, what should I do to inherit eternal life?"

Jesus replied, "What does the law of Moses say? How do you read it?"

The man answered, "'You must love the LORD your God with all your heart, all your soul, all your strength, and all your mind.' And, 'Love your neighbor as yourself.'"

"Right!" Jesus told him. "Do this and you will live!"

The man wanted to justify his actions, so he asked Jesus, "And who is my neighbor?"

Jesus answered by launching into a story. I imagined the scene in vivid detail as Flash paused to pull some tender leaves from a shrub along our path:

A Jewish man was traveling from Jerusalem to Jericho along a route called the "Way of Blood" since so many ruthless bandits attacked people on this stretch of road. Sure enough, some highway bandits ambushed the man. They took his clothes, robbed him, and beat him severely, leaving him by the side of the road.

By chance, a Jewish priest came by.
Did he hear the man moaning and pleading for help?

Instead of stopping, the priest quickly crossed to the other side of the road and kept going. Later, a Temple assistant from Jerusalem noticed the victim lying there, but he offered no assistance before leaving. By now, the injured man was nearly dead.

Then a Samaritan (and Samaritans were deeply despised by the Jews) happened upon the man. He was riding his sure-footed donkey down the road, maybe reviewing what he needed to accomplish once he reached his destination. He had people waiting for him and business to attend to.

If only my donkey would pick up her pace!

But when he saw the man, his plans immediately changed.

Quickly, the Samaritan dismounted his donkey, grabbing a flask of oil. Kneeling down beside the man, the Samaritan tore strips from his own clothing to clean the stranger's wounds and bind them up. The beaten man tried to tell him what had happened, but he could only cough and wince in pain.

"*Shhh.* Don't try to talk," said the compassionate Samaritan. He put his arms around him and lifted him onto his donkey, who looked back at her new passenger, ears pricked with concern.

"We've got several miles to go before we get to Jericho, but I'll hang on to you. My donkey can find the way in her sleep." The Samaritan clicked his tongue, and the donkey began the slow descent into Jericho.

The Samaritan found an inn and stayed with the

man the entire night, changing his bandages and putting cool cloths on his head. In the morning, he handed the innkeeper two silver coins and told him to look after the wounded guest. "If the bill runs higher, I'll settle up when I return," he said.

Jesus looked at the crowd of people listening to the story, then zeroed in on the law expert who had asked, "Who is my neighbor?"

"Now," Jesus said, "which one of the three travelers was a neighbor to this man?"

"The one who showed mercy," said the expert, unable to bring himself to utter the word *Samaritan*.

"Yes. Go now and do the same," Jesus told him.

Mercy and compassion. These were the lenses through which the Samaritan was seeing the man. The priest and the Temple assistant must have left their "mercy glasses" at home that day. Perhaps they were too pressed for time or could not bring themselves to touch someone who looked like he might die any minute: After all, there are rules for this sort of thing. Maybe they thought the man had somehow brought this on himself, or perhaps they worried that stopping would make them vulnerable to attack as well.

There are so many reasons why mercy isn't the "right" answer:

It's inconvenient.

It's expensive.

It could be misconstrued.

He doesn't deserve it.

She isn't the right color.

They practice the wrong religion.
The government should do it.
It's an interruption.

Yes, it *is* an interruption. And yet, interruptions can break open our hearts and reveal what's really inside. They help us see the "other" as a human being, made in the *imago Dei*, the image of God. They strip away what's superfluous and help us get to the very center of how God wants us to live:

> No, O people, the Lord has told you what is good,
>   and this is what he requires of you:
> to do what is right, to love mercy,
>   and to walk humbly with your God.
>
> MICAH 6:8

There is nothing better than stepping into God's stream of compassion. My individualized approach to life—fulfilling my purpose, following my dreams, finding my calling—had kept me occupied and vaguely dissatisfied, all while helping me avoid the deeper, harder work of loving the people right in front of me. And when you love like this, there are no guarantees, no "results" you can count on—only the presence of the Spirit whispering, *This is what it's all about.*

I wish I could say we wrapped up Shonda's story with a neat bow, but her journey is not over yet. We helped her through a tough time, but she impacted us far beyond our year together.

We learned there are no quick fixes or easy answers, especially when compounded by the effects of systemic racism and injustice. Our eyes were opened to a world of hurt and struggle, yet one filled with resilience, joy, and dignity.

When the school year ended, Shonda and the kids found a place to live that was closer to her work, and closer to Meghan and Nathan. Though they are no longer near us, we keep up with the family through e-mail and texts, and they will always have a special place in our hearts.

It wasn't an interruption after all; it was an intervention.

A divine intervention that left me humbled and grateful . . . and changed.

It turns out that meeting interruptions—and all of life—with mercy, openness, and grace is just what God is looking for.

CHAPTER 10
O Gracious Light

O gracious Light,
pure brightness of the everliving
Father in heaven,
O Jesus Christ, holy and blessed!

Now as we come to the setting of the sun,
and our eyes behold the vesper light,
we sing your praises,
O God: Father, Son, and Holy Spirit.

You are worthy at all times
to be praised by happy voices,
O Son of God, O Giver of life,
and to be glorified through all the worlds.

Order for Evening: Rite Two, "O Gracious Light (*Phos hilaron*),"
The Book of Common Prayer

The long shadows of cedar trees pirouetted across Flash and Henry's pasture with the grace of a ballerina. I had hurriedly washed the last dinner dish, then headed to the gate so I wouldn't miss the coming sunset. The descending light danced to the whirring hum of cicadas that had silently emerged from the ground as nymphs, shedding their paper-thin skins on tree trunks and fence posts so they were free to mate.

I wanted to watch the sun make its final bow, throwing theatrical kisses of purple, magenta, pink, orange, and yellow hues into the sky as it exited the stage. The curtain of night would soon close on the day, but not before these last moments of magical in-between time.

Evensong. An Old English ecclesiastical word that befits this golden hour.

Flash and Henry, following their daily protocol, grazed with last-minute intensity like children remembering they need a survival snack before bedtime. Their ability to feel with their lips for the choicest stalks of grass and most delicious bits of leaves never fails to entertain me. Flash's method is refined, his nose and mouth moving along the ground like a fine sensor. He finds the desired clump and closes his lips around it, then delicately bites off the tops with neat precision. Henry, on the other hand, finds his mark with nimble lips, and with a jerk of his head, *rrrips* the grass, roots and all, from the ground. With the longest piece hanging from both sides of his mouth, he begins to pull it in—bite by bite. The juicy tip disappears into his mouth first; then just as the root nears the other corner of his mouth, he bites and lets it fall to the ground. He's such a messy eater, leaving a wake of grass destruction behind everywhere he goes. This evening was no exception.

I skirted around a cactus toward Henry and held out my still-damp hand. He shook his ears and avoided my gaze, intent on obliterating another clump of sparse grass. When given the choice between attention or food in the remaining minutes of daylight, food always wins.

I rested my hand on Henry's shoulder and brushed off the tiny bits of grass that clung to his smooth coat from his last roll on the ground. The gentle sounds coming from the pasture and the two grazing donkeys slowed my breaths. Step, rustle, rip, chew, step, repeat. A swish of a tail, a shake of the ears, a quiet *pphhh*. Crickets jumped this way and that, catching the attention of a loitering cattle egret who was seizing his evening snack too. There was a flap of white wings as the bird lifted into the air, then landed, wings folding and eyes alert to the next insect. A mockingbird perched on a fence post, posing first in one direction, then another, confident each side was his best. His clear notes on the heavy air seemed to echo off the line of cedars at the edge of the pasture and return to fall into the field. A young cottontail rabbit appeared from behind a scrubby tree, taking two or three hops before seeing me and freezing, assessing its options.

"Hey there, little bun-bun." My voice was quiet and sing-songy. "It's okay; you can keep hopping." I thought that giving permission might be helpful. He sat perfectly still; only his nose twitched. Then, in two quick leaps, his white tail puff disappeared from view.

Turning to face west, I inhaled the scent of the mealy sage and bluestem grass and took in the fading blue sky. Everything was bathed in soft sunlight, all golden and magic. Small clouds settled on the rim of the horizon, as if preparing to bed down for the night.

O gracious Light . . .

The Liturgy of the Hours, an ancient practice of prayer, was doing a number on me. When I discovered it, I'd found myself drawn to its simple beauty. Sometimes called fixed hour prayer, the Daily Office, the Divine Office, or my favorite, *Opus Dei* (the Work of God), it's one of the oldest forms of spiritual discipline and can trace its roots to Judaism, from which Christianity came. Until recently, I'd been completely unaware of anything called *spiritual discipline*. When I first heard the term, I rejected it out of hand for what sounded like religiosity. The last thing I wanted (or needed) was to add a layer of "have tos" in my life. After all, didn't Jesus set us free from all that?

And yet . . . I was intrigued. The Hours gave me a structured way to "pray without ceasing." I felt strengthened by the constancy of morning, midday, and evening liturgies. Evening prayers, called vespers, could be followed by compline, the service that "completes" the day.

To be honest, sometimes I completely forgot to pray. I'd wake up and launch into the day, not stopping until I fell into bed that night. Other days I would sit on the couch and pray the morning prayers only, or I'd open a browser on my phone and find the evening prayers just before nodding off to sleep. After years of trying—and failing—to pray regularly, the sacred rhythm of the Hours was a lifeline that connected me to a framework and focus, directing my thoughts toward God. My personal prayers for family and situations on my heart were being rooted in fertile spiritual soil.

I began to recognize that certain prayers within the liturgy were making their appearances with regularity, and I soon became more acquainted with them. As the months passed, I was pleased to find that our acquaintanceship was becoming a real friendship. As with any new relationship, I found it was important not to force things but to let this one develop naturally. One must allow new friends to reveal themselves in their own time and manner.

Well, hello there, my friend! The prayers came softly, as the best of friends often do.

"O Gracious Light (*Phos hilaron*)," part of the vespers liturgy, captivated me from the start. Beautifully poetic, it evokes wonder. As I researched the ancient hymn's history and breathed its words each night, I fell in love with the way it disclosed God in the phrases, opening my heart to Him in a new way. "O Gracious Light" is the oldest known hymn of the church (outside of Scripture itself) still being sung today. Originally written in Koine Greek in the late third or early fourth century, the song has been translated into many languages over time.

The English reads like this:

> *O gracious Light,*
> *pure brightness of the everliving Father in heaven,*
> *O Jesus Christ, holy and blessed!*

Now as we come to the setting of the sun,
and our eyes behold the vesper light,
we sing your praises,
O God: Father, Son, and Holy Spirit.

You are worthy at all times to be praised by happy voices,
O Son of God, O Giver of life,
and to be glorified through all the worlds.

I particularly love the Lutheran version:

Joyous light of glory of the immortal Father,
Heavenly, holy, blessed Jesus Christ,
We have come to the setting of the Sun
And we look to the evening light.
We sing to God, the Father, the Son and Holy Spirit.
You are worthy of being praised with pure voices forever.
O Son of God, O Giver of Light,
The universe proclaims your glory.

I would never have been able to pray such lyrical words on my own without the sense I was putting on airs. I mean, here I was standing in a dusty pasture with two long-eared donkeys after washing greasy lasagna dishes. *I need a shower, come to think of it.*

Yes, I would have felt like such a fraud had I tried to make up this kind of lofty language. Yet reading the ancient words, breathing them, offering them . . . oh, they were exactly what my soul wanted to say.

The universe proclaims your glory.

Here and now, in this in-between time.

The sunset did not disappoint. The light slid lower on the horizon, momentarily turning Henry's ear tufts into golden flags that fluttered with each movement. The last rays tinged his chocolate hair with red highlights, the dark cross emblazoned across his shoulders even more pronounced than usual. He paused his chewing long enough to look up at me, then out toward the setting sun, grass still protruding from the corners of his mouth. *Oh, Henry, always with your mouth full.*

We both exhaled at the same time, my little donkey and me, sharing the contentment of the moment. I gave him a final ear scratch, called good night to Flash, and turned toward the house to gather supplies for the next day's art project.

^ ^

My painting jobs were getting fewer and farther between, but I still had some favorite clients who continued to call me when they had a decorative project in mind. One was expecting a baby and asked if I could please, please, please stop being selfish about writing for a few days so I could paint her nursery?

I laughed. How could I refuse?

But first things first: early morning chores. I watered the flower beds around the house, scooped donkey manure from the barn area, and prepared hay for "the boys," who were still out in the pasture. Henry always arrived at the barn first, with Flash lumbering sleepily behind. As I set out their separate piles of hay, they selected the one nearest them and plunged in. Well, Henry plunged in, breaking the flake apart with his hoof for maximum fluff. Flash nibbled off the top of his and looked at Henry before giving me a knowing glance. *He still has food issues, huh?*

As if on cue, both donkeys stopped eating and eyed the other's hay. Ears back, Flash bobbed his head and blew. Henry tilted his head and lowered his eyes. *Trade ya!* they mimed, immediately switching places. Each apparently satisfied that now they had gotten the better deal, Flash and Henry settled in for their meal like a couple of brothers.

When I finally arrived at my client's house, I unpacked my painting supplies, climbed the ladder, and set to work on a farm scene along one wall of the nursery. In the distance, I had decided to feature a red barn on a hill with a menagerie of farm animals—a cow, a horse, pigs, and chickens. In the foreground, green grass along the bottom edge of the wall would lead the eye to a large oak tree (with a swing) near the corner of the room.

Starting with outlines of the general shapes, I began to block in the colors but then decided to focus on the tree: trunk, branches, and leaves. I love acrylic paints because they're so forgiving. Working from the background to the foreground, they allow me to paint over mistakes until I'm happy with the result. I need this kind of medium; without it, my perfectionist tendencies would probably paralyze me.

With a two-inch brush, I used my darkest greens to scrub in what would become the shadowy leaves, knowing that I didn't have to work much detail into them. Next came the medium-toned green, the main color of the foliage. Now I paid more attention to the shapes of the leaves by using smaller, more refined brushes. It took almost the entire day just to get the scene to the point of looking treeish, but it still seemed flat and lifeless on the wall. I sat back on a ladder step and stared at the painting, squinting a little to help me imagine how to finish it. Right on cue, self-doubt crept in. *It looks like garbage. Your client will hate this whole mural when she comes home and sees it half-done. Also, you have no talent.*

My inner critic is cruel like that.

Experience, however, has taught me to ignore this voice and just keep going.

This tree just needed some deeper shadows—and highlights. Definitely highlights.

By the time I began adding blobs of light green and citron to the leaves, my inner critic had turned sheepish and was off in a corner. The tree was coming to life. Dark shadows gave it depth and shape, and those highlights made it pop. It was as if the sun were kissing each leaf, brightly transforming the entire tree into something beautiful.

I took a sip of the iced coffee I'd brought along and considered the shadows and light in my own life. *Penny and Prince.* The shadows of sadness and guilt still welled up inside me from time to time. I wondered about what might have been and how everything could have turned out so differently. I wanted to go back in time for a do-over. And yet . . . I knew that *because* of what happened, we now had Henry, a joyful light. I couldn't imagine life without him. One of my worst moments had brought about one of the best gifts.

Shadows and light.

That combination can make all the difference in art—*and* in life. I had spent so much time wishing I could flatten out the highs and lows in order to manage everything better. *If only I could skip all the drama!* Yet those highs and lows were the very things giving meaning and texture to my existence. If everything were "nothing-too-hard" and "nothing-too-exciting,"

I might certainly be able to live efficiently, but I would miss the whole experience of what it means to be human.

My phone buzzed with an incoming text from Tom.

"Henry got out."

What??

Then this one:

"Doggone it. I don't have time for this."

Oh dear. How could Henry have gotten out? I tried calling Tom, but he didn't pick up.

Then . . .

"Never mind—got him."

Whew, crisis averted.

A little while later, another text:

"H out again [mad-face emoji]."

There wasn't much I could do from my job site, so I crossed my fingers and hoped Tom could just catch him and figure out how to keep him from escaping.

"Squeezed under gate."

Squeezed under gate? How in the world? . . .

Aahh. Just then it all began to make sense. I started laughing so hard I nearly fell off the ladder.

When I checked on the donkeys' water the night before, I had noticed Henry doing what looked like a downward-facing-dog yoga pose near the salt block. Front legs stretched forward, head down, tail end up in the air.

I chuckled at the ridiculous sight.

"Henry, what are you doing?" I teased him. He responded by standing and bringing his left back leg up to his nose in a revolved-side-angle pose.

"Oh. My. Goodness. Henry, you're a nut," I told him, putting my hands on both sides of his head and planting a kiss on his velvety nose. I wiggled my fingers into his cheeks, scratching until his eyes closed.

Now, with Tom's texts, I realized Henry had been warming up for a Big Escape under the gate. With only about an eighteen-inch clearance, he would need to employ his downward-facing-dog move, bring his back feet under the gate with a high lunge, and push forward to stand on the other side.

Mountain pose.

For all his idiosyncrasies, Henry made my heart glad.

We sing your praises, O God . . .

I climbed higher on the ladder to reach the top of the oak tree, where it needed a bit more shadow to make the leaves stand out. *Hmmm, that's better.*

Looking around the nursery, I saw a white crib, a changing table, and adorable outfits that were awaiting the newborn's arrival. It was so perfect and welcoming. My heart lurched in my chest and my smile faded as I remembered the nursery I'd once planned, the one that never received my own newborn baby.

Grief had consumed me at age forty when I lost a pregnancy in a car accident, a baby I desperately wanted. I was overcome with such sorrow that it felt impossible to function. I was angry with God, mad at myself for running a silly errand that put me at the wrong place at the wrong time, and confused by the conflicting messages people gave me, intending to bring comfort. Fourteen years on, I still ached for my child and wondered at "what could have been."

The anger I held is gone these days, and so is the sharp grief that once resided right under the surface of my heart—at least until I hear of someone who's lost a baby. Then I can't help but let the tears fall, and I feel the weight on my chest. I'm left with memories that linger in the corners, reminding me that loss will always be part of my soul. Yet because of it, I'm deeply connected to all the women who have lived and longed for babies they, too, never got to cradle. I am part of a precious sisterhood, and I hold it close.

Time—and light—have brought beauty to the pain.

The shadows have a way of throwing into relief the play and sparkle of light, enhancing our joyous experiences in ways we can't put into words. I have grandbabies now—our daughters are fully immersed in their own motherhood journey—and the delight these little ones bring me is unlike anything else I could imagine. Ivy, Heidi, Hazel, August, and Caroline arrived one after the other; kisses of sunlight that absolutely rock my world, made all the more precious against the backdrop of pain.

Our eyes behold the vesper light . . .

I realize, of course, that sunlight can be explained in scientific terms. I'm just nerdy enough to know that its rays are born when tiny photons leave the fiery ball of burning gas we call the sun, travel through space, and reach the earth in the span of eight minutes. Photons, at the level of quantum particles, behave in ways that seem to defy logic. They become particles or they become waves depending on whether they are being observed. Huh? Does that make sense to you?

Likewise, consider this interesting tidbit about electrons: "If you know where an electron is you cannot, by definition, know where it is going. If you know where it is going, you cannot know where it is. Furthermore, you cannot know any of these things without interacting with them, which means that you will never know how they behave when you are not watching."

Some may speculate (as I do) that all creation is being watched over, not least of all the light. Though the origins of light are scientifically complex, to me it is simply . . . wondrous, inviting us to see our world in a new way. As the sun's rays pass through the atmosphere, they create the golden glow and colors of the sunset that, from our vantage point, soften the hard edges of our earthly reality.

After finishing for the day, I pulled up in front of Beulah, got out of the Suburban, and stood in the evening light before going inside. I reviewed my world—an old house that needs repair, a dusty pasture, a vehicle full of ladders and paint supplies, a stack of bills on the desk, children now grown, two donkeys with attitudes—I was struck with the beauty of all it contained. None of it was perfect, and yet bathed in light particles, it was achingly good.

It occurred to me then: If we could only look at the world while standing in the light of Jesus!

In His light, *His gracious light*, we can see light everywhere, even in the brokenness that surrounds us. The first chapter of John's Gospel so beautifully expresses that Jesus is "the true Light . . . coming into the world . . . that illumines every person." His light is at work in all creation and in the life of every human being, no matter how broken they may be. Perhaps it's as songwriter Leonard Cohen put it: "There is a crack in everything / That's how the light gets in."

Thousands of years ago, the psalmist David wrote, "You cause them to drink of the stream of Your pleasures. For with You is the fountain of life; in Your light do we see light." The sacred words ring in our hearts.

As we gaze upon the countenance of Christ, we will bathe in His gracious light, which gladdens our hearts and compels us to praise Him.

CHAPTER II

The Way of Peace

Blessed be the Lord, the God of Israel;
he has come to his people and set them free.
He has raised up for us a mighty savior,
born of the house of his servant David. . . .
In the tender compassion of our God
the dawn from on high shall break upon us,
To shine on those who dwell in darkness and the shadow of death,
and to guide our feet into the way of peace.

Glory to the Father, and to the Son, and to the Holy Spirit:
as it was in the beginning, is now, and will be for ever. Amen.

Daily Morning Prayer: Rite Two, from "The Song of Zechariah
(*Benedictus Dominus Deus*): Luke 1:68-79,"
The Book of Common Prayer

couldn't wait to tell Flash.

"You've been invited to an event as guest of honor!"

Flash didn't seem surprised one bit, as if to say, *Well, you didn't expect they'd pick Henry, did you?*

The occasion would be hosted by Paws for Reflection Ranch, a local therapeutic animal facility. So local, in fact, that it was only a half mile from our house—close enough for us to walk rather than borrow a horse trailer. Of course, Henry would accompany Flash—that is, if the two donkeys would agree to the walk down our country road.

"I don't know about this," Tom said as I handed him Flash's halter and rope.

"I think they'll do fine," I replied with a confident air. "Henry is really coming along on his walking skills, and if they're together, they should cooperate with us." I employed my best chipper tone in an effort to convince him.

"There are too many variables here," said the pessimist in the ball cap. "They've never walked on pavement, there are too many other strange surfaces to walk over, there's all kinds of tasty green grass, the cars and trucks will go too fast, the dogs will bark . . . and you have not fooled me into believing that Henry will walk in anything but reverse. This is going to be a nightmare." He gave me *his* look that said *I don't know how you talk me into doing this stuff for you.*

"Relax. I've given us plenty of time to get there, and I have baggies of sweet feed and carrots for us to use." I pretended Tom's assessment hadn't rattled me as I fitted Henry's blue halter over his head. Brushed until they glistened and outfitted with coordinating green bandanas around their necks, the two donkeys looked like celebrities. I knew they'd be a hit with the ranch guests—if only we could get them there.

"You lead," I directed Tom, "and we'll follow. Let's try to be patient with them. It's a new experience, so I know they won't be perfect." Lowering our expectations was essential.

Tom gave Flash a bear hug around his neck and whispered in his ear, no doubt giving him a pep talk. "Okay, Flashy. Walk on!" Tom stepped out ahead, while Flash watched him walk to the end of the slackened rope and jerk to a full stop. Flash hadn't moved a muscle, as unbudging as a ship's anchor.

"Really?" Tom gave the lead rope a small tug to insist on cooperation. Flash ignored him and turned around to look back at Henry. He was busy in midrotation.

"Oh, for crying out loud, Henry." I tried to maneuver his head around to face me, but I was no match. He extended a back foot and inched in my direction.

Dear Lord, have mercy. This is going to take. for. ever.

Flash used this standstill to examine his life, perhaps thinking about the bees that buzzed in the adjacent field. *Are those honeybees or bumblebees? Is there a difference? Because they seem so alike.*

Apparently, you can't rush the donkey thought process.

Tom's gaze darted, skimming over one donkey at a dead stop and the other facing backward. His eyes stopped and took clear aim at me: *I told you so.*

Mine immediately shot back: *I don't need your comments.*

Henry glanced at me over his shoulder and lifted his tail.

No! Do not explode right now! Not a good time, Henry!

"Come on, bud. You can do this. Walk on . . ." is what I actually said, calmly and collectedly. Lowering his tail, Henry grabbed a mouthful of grass and began to chew, as if this whole exercise were about breakfast.

Flash wrapped up his contemplation. *Yep, honeybees.* He swished his tail, nodded his head, and started to walk.

Henry weighed his options. Once again, he glanced over his shoulder and saw that Flash was leaving. Ears moving, he reluctantly figured he might as well join in. His back leg stretched out behind him—first one, then the other.

At this rate, we might be there for the closing ceremonies.

"It's okay, buddy. Just turn around when you can—no rush."

Finally, rotating 180, Henry turned to face me and fell into step as we paraded down the road—Tom, Flash, me, and Henry.

Still only a half mile to go, minus maybe ten steps.

The grass along the way was supertempting and conveniently accessible. Henry did pretty well as long as Flash kept going. Every now and then, Flash had to stop and ponder. *What? Branches overhead? Scary! And why are those cars speeding by?*

Each stop required patience on the humans' part and also required that Henry repeat his ritual: A slow turn to face backward. A stop to think and look at where he'd been. A moment of worry about being left behind, then a check to see if Flash had started moving. Finally, a response to my tug on the lead by inching forward . . . in reverse. After several backward steps, he'd stop again, then slowly turn to face forward before walking on—as if all this were normal.

Will we make it to the event on time? Each stop triggered one of my hot flashes and tested my antiperspirant. Each stop made me think of Jesus—dear Jesus, trying to make his way into Jerusalem on the back of a greenhorn donkey colt, riding over uneven palm branches and scattered cloaks to the deafening roar of a cheering crowd. What a risky way to make a "Triumphal Entry." It could have ended in complete embarrassment.

Yes, this is what you think about when you're trying to get somewhere on time with a donkey.

Walking with donkeys just for the fun of it is quite enjoyable. Walking with donkeys with a goal in mind is another thing altogether—it's fraught with anxiety. Maybe Jesus, like Tom and me, had given Himself plenty of time.

Zechariah prophesied how Jesus' event would unfold:

Rejoice, O people of Zion!
    Shout in triumph, O people of Jerusalem!
Look, your king is coming to you.
    He is righteous and victorious,
yet he is humble, riding on a donkey—
    riding on a donkey's colt.
I will remove the battle chariots from Israel
    and the warhorses from Jerusalem.
I will destroy all the weapons used in battle,
    and your king will bring peace to the nations.
His realm will stretch from sea to sea
    and from the Euphrates River to the ends of
        the earth.

ZECHARIAH 9:9-10

Scholars have argued over whether Jesus' journey included one donkey or two. It's not exactly clear since Matthew's account differs from the other Gospels. But the key to the success of His venture, in my opinion, wasn't the lure of carrots; it was that the colt's mother led the way. Ask any donkey owner, and they will assure you: An inexperienced colt would have needed a lead donkey to follow. An untested donkey without a trusted leader would have balked at the first sight of something unfamiliar on the ground, at a raucous crowd pressing in.

Stepping over cloaks and branches? Unthinkable.

People shouting and waving their arms? Frightening.

Yep. There were definitely two donkeys.

What a sight Jesus must have been! A grown man straddling a small donkey, his feet nearly touching the ground as the animal stepped skittishly into the city.

This was no fancy warhorse.

This was a peace donkey.

A peace donkey that, in all likelihood, couldn't have made it without his mama nearby.

As Jesus crested the hill to descend into the city, the crowds must have immediately thought of Zechariah's Old Testament prophecy and believed it was coming to pass before their very eyes. But they mistook Jesus' Triumphal Entry as a political coup—the end of Roman tyranny, the restoration of the Jewish kingdom. *Is this the moment we take Israel back for God?*

The event was not lost on the religious leaders either. However, rather than seeing Jesus' Triumphal Entry as a fulfillment of biblical prophecy, they saw it as a theatrical mockery.

They were enraged. *How dare he? How dare he ride on a donkey? Who does he think he is?*

In the New Testament, Zechariah, a Jewish priest and father of John the Baptist, is one of many who witnessed the unfolding events prophesied by the Zechariah of the Old Testament. As John's father held his newborn son, he, too, delivered a prophecy that resounded with Scripture's promise: Peace would arrive with the coming Messiah. Zechariah's prophecy is the same prayer that opened this chapter. Seeing it show up time and again in my daily liturgy called my attention to its message.

The same questions that swirled around Jesus echo through our own world today—or at least in my world. *Did Jesus come to establish a political kingdom, or something quite different? What does it look like to be a Christ follower in our twenty-first-century world?* I was still "moving the furniture around" in my head to understand it all.

In the past few years, it had felt like I'd somehow been soaking in a mixed marinade that was one part evangelical and two parts cable news. Throw in a generous pinch of social media, and it was hard to tell where Christianity left off and angry politics began. *Is this how Jesus' Kingdom is supposed to be?* I wondered. Certain things were not adding up for me.

> *In the tender compassion of our*
> *God the dawn from on high*
> *shall break upon us . . .*

Recently, I'd forced myself to turn off the news and television commentaries and go back to soaking in the narratives of the Gospels. I gravitated to the Beatitudes, the crown jewel of Jesus' famous Sermon on the Mount.

> God blesses those who are poor and realize their
>   need for him,
>   for the Kingdom of Heaven is theirs.
> God blesses those who mourn,
>   for they will be comforted.
> God blesses those who are humble,
>   for they will inherit the whole earth.
> God blesses those who hunger and thirst for justice,
>   for they will be satisfied.
> God blesses those who are merciful,
>   for they will be shown mercy.
> God blesses those whose hearts are pure,
>   for they will see God.
> God blesses those who work for peace,
>   for they will be called the children of God.
> God blesses those who are persecuted for doing right,
>   for the Kingdom of Heaven is theirs.
>
> MATTHEW 5:3-10

If Jesus is going to build a successful Kingdom, I mused, *it surely won't be through the kind of people He described as blessed—poor, mourning, humble, justice seeking, merciful, pure hearted, peacemaking, and persecuted.* Not many of the leadership books I'd read listed these attributes as hallmarks for changing the world. Perhaps I'd just grown weary of the warrior motifs, the standard "soldiers for Christ" messages that seemed to pack pews and sell books, yet felt far from the peaceable Kingdom Jesus had described.

Something in my heart was changing. I wanted a Jesus who rode a donkey, not one who waged war on a culture indifferent to our evangelical moral outrage. I resonated with Eugene Peterson's perspective:

> The Christian life is the lifelong practice of attending
> to the details of congruence—congruence between
> ends and means, congruence between what we do
> and the way we do it, congruence between what is
> written in Scripture and our living out what is written,
> congruence between a ship and its prow, congruence
> between preaching and living, congruence between
> the sermon and what is lived in both preacher and
> congregation, the congruence of the Word made
> flesh in Jesus with what is lived in our flesh.

Jesus had always been a puzzle to me. As a child, I remember asking my Sunday school teacher why we didn't sell our possessions and give to the poor, or turn the other cheek instead of retaliate, or love our enemies rather than kill them. I was told, in the most loving way, that we were to take Jesus' teachings and balance them with the rest of Scripture. They were more "philosophical" than literal, meant to show us we could never attain the perfection that only His death on the cross could accomplish for us. His teachings weren't intended to be taken at face value. This explanation for me began a lifetime of trying to keep Jesus' radical Kingdom at a safe distance from the more "practical" ways of living.

Incongruence. Maybe that's what was bothering me.

I said I was a Christ follower, but in truth I was an American

Ideals follower. I prized its work ethic, independence, national pride, and swagger. But I came to see that Jesus, whose Kingdom transcends time and space, is about something more profound.

Why would Jesus risk his Triumphal Entry by riding a borrowed, inexperienced donkey? Why not take this opportunity to parade in on a regal Arabian steed, a mark of esteem and power?

Jesus was making a statement about the kind of Kingdom He was establishing—one not denoted by military might, intimidation, earthly power, and coercion, but by love, peace, gentleness, and humility.

His Kingdom is marked by beauty, "a beauty that will save the world."

This is the kind of Kingdom worth living for. It's the kind of Kingdom that was captivating my heart.

"Look, your king is coming to you . . . humble, riding on a donkey."

To guide our feet into the
way of peace . . .

This is how God's Kingdom comes.
Humbly.
Quietly.
Peacefully.

"Bring Flash and Henry into the arena at noon so we can introduce them to our guests in the stands," Melode, the ranch director, instructed me. The donkeys had successfully walked to the ranch and gone into the pen set up for them! Yes, it had taken thirty minutes to walk the half mile from our pasture, but I was intensely proud of their efforts.

"With due respect, I think we should quit while we're ahead," I told her. "Tom left to get some work done at the office, and I don't know if they'll walk with anyone else. Plus, they've never been in a horse arena, never set foot in soft sand, and never stood in front of a crowd. This has all the makings of an epic failure."

Melode laughed. "Well, let's see what happens. If it doesn't work, we'll just bring them back to the pen. I have confidence."

I was glad somebody did. I glanced at the donkeys, who both wore distinct *We're done here* expressions. You know—the kind of stares that just dare you to suggest something new.

Nonetheless, at the appointed time, Melode and I haltered up Flash and Henry, adjusted their bandanas, and led them to the arena. Lo and behold, there were no incidents, and Henry even walked forward! They'd paused only momentarily at the deep sand covering the ground; yet miraculously, they proceeded to walk in like professionals!

We stopped in the middle, where I handed Henry off to one of Melode's helpers so I could make my way to the microphone. I told the stories behind these rescue animals and explained how they had impacted me in a profound way. And then . . . the crowd erupted in laughter.

Did I say something funny?

I looked over, and there was Henry on his back, belly up and rolling side to side with joyful abandon while Flash looked on indulgently. Sand flew in all directions as Henry rubbed his back and kicked his feet, his little tail a broom brushing back and forth.

Oh, Henry, why now?

As if we had rehearsed it, he leapt to his feet, shook his long ears, and gave a huge yawn that resembled a silly grin. The audience applauded in delight.

A peace donkey had stolen the show.

Something special happens when a donkey helps people let down their guard: They smile. They open their hearts. They become vulnerable. They know there is nothing to fear from an animal whose very nature seeks to bear burdens and to serve.

In our rapid-fire, success-driven lives, it's easy to forget the Kingdom comes slowly, humbly, and peaceably through people whose lives, though imperfect, are marked by sacrifice and love in the image of the Cross.

The gospel of Jesus—ushered in on a lowly donkey whose inexperience could have easily let Him down—is not only beautiful; it is also the way of peace.

CHAPTER 12

Companion in the Way

Lord Jesus, stay with us,
for evening is at hand and the day is past;
be our companion in the way,
kindle our hearts, and awaken hope,
that we may know you
as you are revealed in Scripture
and the breaking of bread.
Grant this for the sake of your love. Amen.

Daily Evening Prayer: Rite Two, "A Collect for the Presence of Christ,"
The Book of Common Prayer

"*HEE-haw, hee-HAW, heeeeee!*"

I heard him long before I could see him.

"*HAW, haw, HEE-EEE!*" Henry's high-pitched bray was unmistakable, but I'd never heard him sound so panicked. The chubby little donkey galloped around the corner of the barn, ears up and eyes wide in terror. He thundered to a stop in front of me, wheezed, and turned to run back in the direction he'd just come from.

Skidding to a stop near the trees edging the woods, he wheeled around again and headed back—full speed. He halted in front of me, spun in a circle, and once again took off toward the woods, this time looking back and braying as he went.

He was acting exactly like Lassie of TV and movie fame.

Henry is trying to tell me something. Henry wants me to follow him!

"Oh no, Flash must be in danger!" I sprinted after Henry, looking in all directions for the bigger donkey.

This can't be good. My heart started beating uncomfortably fast.

"Flash! Flashy!" I yelled as loudly as possible. By now I was making my way into the woods on one of Flash's self-made trails. All was completely silent except for birds flitting in the treetops. The main donkey trail was well used and branched into smaller trails throughout the forest floor, which was otherwise a mess of downed tree limbs, twigs, leaves, and vines. Even on the trails, it was impossible to walk without rustling the leaves on the bushes or breaking some twigs underfoot.

I stopped to listen but could only hear Henry's heavy breathing beside me. If Flash was moving about, I'd surely hear him crashing through the underbrush.

Nothing.

I called and waited. Called and waited.

Flash must be in another part of the pasture.

I tried to control my own rising panic as I fumbled for my phone and called Tom.

"We might have a small emergency," I said before my composure broke. "*Get out here right away!*"

He arrived within minutes, and I briefed him. Together we checked all the pasture gates and did several sweeps of the entire six-acre pasture and woods while Henry followed us, bawling.

Flash was gone.

He might be dead somewhere.

My heart thudded, and everything that had happened with Penny and Prince came crashing over me. *No, Lord. Please, no.*

Henry was now beside himself. Braying and pooping and running, he wasn't listening to a thing we said to calm him down. This was a disaster: One donkey was gone, and the other was losing his marbles over it.

"I'm going to widen the search to the rest of the property and make sure the driveway gate is closed," Tom told me. "Stay with Henderson, because he'll totally freak out if we leave him alone now."

I looked at Henry. His lower lip was trembling, and his head drooped almost to the ground—all that crying and running had worn him out. My heart went out to him. As often as he and Flash had their differences, I hadn't realized just how much Henry needed his companion. He couldn't live without him.

I knelt down next to the little donkey and prayed. "Dear Lord, help us find Flash!" Henry's bowed head came up, and he looked at me with a pleading expression. *Oh, please find my friend.*

I decided to make one last slow pass through the woods. It was hard to believe Flash could be there, but it was the only logical place where we might have missed him. His brown-gray coat blended with the trees and brush, so it was possible he was lying down, perfectly camouflaged. Maybe he'd been hit by a falling branch, or had fallen into a hole, or . . .

My imagination was starting to get the best of me.

Swallowing hard, I retraced my steps, stopping a few yards in. "Flash! Flash!" I waited for some telltale noise.

Nothing. The minutes passed with no sign of him.

Suddenly, I felt a nudge on my arm. *What in the world?*

Flash had materialized right next to me, without a sound! I turned to face him. He seemed to shrug as though nothing were amiss, then bent and scratched his nose on his foreleg, real casual-like.

At that moment, I knew what he'd been up to.

He'd been hiding. Hiding from Henry.

Henry bellowed his distress from the pasture, and Flash looked at me more intently. He gave the most resigned sigh I'd ever heard and shook his ears, as though today he couldn't bear to face the neediness—dear Lord, the *neediness*!

I understood. "Aw, Flash! You just needed some time to yourself! I don't blame you." I gave him a knuckle-rub on his forehead to let him know I'd keep his secret. Flash offered an appreciative snort, then nodded his head as he gathered himself up to go out and pretend he hadn't heard all of Henry's bellyaching.

Flash and I emerged from the woods to find Henry mid-bray: eyes closed and head back, just hee-hawing away. When he opened his eyes and saw us, he immediately shut his mouth and stared in disbelief. He trotted right over toward Flash, and I fully expected him to stand up on his hind legs, throw his front legs around his buddy's neck, and weep tears of joy.

Instead . . .

Henry stopped several feet away from Flash and turned his head to look at a nearby tree. He swished his tail while appearing extremely fascinated by its leaves. *My, my, those leaves are certainly stunning today. Just look at those leaves!* He acted like he couldn't care less that his friend had suddenly returned from the dead.

Flash glanced at me with what looked like an eye roll. *So much drama, this one.*

Another big sigh.

"You guys okay here?" I asked. "Henry, you're cool? Flash, you too?"

Flash gave me a nod, an "all cool here" signal. Henry seemed to tell Flash, *Oh, hey. I wasn't even looking for you.* He continued to pretend he had never cried, never ran around in sheer panic. Flash, for his part, continued to pretend he had never heard anything at all.

I gave them two thumbs-up. "Check on you guys later."

Those two. Gotta love 'em.

I couldn't count the number of times I'd just about given up and called Doc Darlin to come get his naughty little Henderson

Number Ten so Flash could live all alone again. It would be so much easier that way, and I knew Flash would be perfectly fine with it.

True, their bickering over food had subsided somewhat, but it wasn't completely tranquil dining. Their "play" was still too rough for my taste. And now we had Flash pulling a disappearing act on us. I mean, how much could a person take?

Still, Henry had come so far, and so had Flash. They were now companions and friends. And I had learned to stop trying to control them and let donkeys be donkeys.

Maybe there was a lesson in that. It's just that I couldn't always tell from their behavior whether they really loved each other. If their inside emotions were warm, their outside actions rarely showed it.

I thought back to an incident at Vacation Bible School when my daughters were small. "Jungle Adventure" was the theme that year, and the church stage had been transformed into an Amazon rain forest, complete with palm trees, cargo crates, and stuffed toy toucans and monkeys in the trees. Someone had even donated a gorilla costume, stuffed with crumpled newspapers to make it more lifelike, and propped it up in the corner.

On the final day, all the children were to gather in the sanctuary for the big finale. Someone had the brilliant idea that I should secretly put on the gorilla costume and sit in the corner. Then, on cue, I would "come to life" and dance with the cast to the week's theme song.

I was totally up for that! Sitting in a gorilla suit, in Texas in July . . . completely motionless until the music starts to play . . . deserves a Tony nomination, even without a dance. Still, I agreed to do it.

When it was finally time for me to move, I stood up. The littlest kids in the front row shrieked in terror, and the bigger kids behind them started to cheer. Soon the whole place was going crazy over this gorilla-come-to-life who was dancing with the cast members. And wow—when I moonwalked, they went wild! It was a huge hit.

Afterward, we all gathered for a group photo—with me still in costume, right in the middle.

The photographer gave us the usual countdown: "3, 2, 1, SMILE!" It took several shots to get one she was happy with, but I gave my biggest and best smile each time.

It wasn't until the final camera click that I caught myself.

Wait. Why am I smiling? No one can see me behind this mask!

It wouldn't have mattered if I'd stuck out my tongue or crossed my eyes; my gorilla expression remained frozen—an enigmatic face that offered no clue of what was behind it. I laughed hysterically, but (not surprisingly) nobody even noticed.

And so it was with Flash and Henry. What was really going on behind those donkey masks? Did Flash just feign his annoyance for the sake of his pride? Henry had already leaked his concern for Flash but then tried to cover it up. Was there any hope I could discover where they truly stood with each other?

^ ^

"Hey, Rach!" I heard my friend Priscilla's voice from the direction of the gate. She had brought her youngest son, Jude, over to pet the donkeys one afternoon while his older brothers finished up their homework.

Happy for an excuse to catch up with one another, I ran into the kitchen and grabbed some carrots so Jude could feed Flash and Henry. Their carrot radar system had already directed them to wait next to the fence.

"Go ahead and give Flash a carrot first, Jude. Then while he's eating, walk down along the fence a little way and give Henry one," I instructed. "He's not big enough to reach over the fence, so just stick the carrot through the wire mesh between you."

Flash's head jutted over the fence, his lips flapping in anticipation. Henry's nose was smooshed against the wire fence, giving him a lopsided donkey grin.

I could see Jude's hesitation. He was only seven years old and hadn't spent as much time with the donkeys as his brothers had. "Um, may I stick the carrot through the fence for Flash, too?" he asked.

"Of course. That way you can keep your fingers away from his nibbles," I told him.

Then Jude had an idea. "How about if I feed Henry and *you* feed Flash?"

"Even better," I said.

Jude took his handful of baby carrots and lured Henry away from us. He giggled as Henry grasped each small carrot with his lips and crunched it eagerly.

Priscilla watched Jude and Henry for a moment, then turned to me as I offered Flash a carrot. "Are you doing okay?" she asked. This time, I didn't squirm. Over the past months, I'd finally begun to share with her snippets of this journey that had me starting over in my faith. I'd been nervous. Admitting there were questions and doubts behind my mask of Christian confidence wasn't easy for me. To my relief, Priscilla had offered a listening ear and given me space to divulge my heart without any judgment. She encouraged me to keep going on this path.

"I'm doing better," I laughed. "Although I feel like I'm putting a jigsaw puzzle back together without a picture on the box to look at!"

"I have something for you," Priscilla replied, reaching into her bag. She pulled out a slim book and placed it in my hands.

"Oh my goodness! What is this?"

"It's a book of prayers written by a Scottish theologian about a hundred years ago," she said. "I love the written prayers you've introduced me to, so when I ran across this gem, I knew I had to order another to pass along to you." The book contained a month's worth of morning and evening prayers . . . but more than that, it contained the thoughtfulness of a friend who knew just how much it would mean to me. *Your story is safe with me.*

An understanding friend isn't always easy to find. Experience has taught me it's risky to be vulnerable. Once, I had cautiously shared an insecurity with a friend, who immediately walked into the next room to gather a group of people to pray for me about my issue—about which she told them in detail. I was mortified. *I'll never do that again,* I thought, looking around for a hole to crawl into.

Lord Jesus, stay with us. . . .
Be our companion in the way . . .

These words from the liturgy sound a little needy, and I'm impatient with my sense of need. I want to have it all together, or at least look like I have it all together.

But maybe neediness is just as it should be.

Sometimes, we need companionship more than we need immediate fixing. We need God's presence more than we need a miracle. We need to know we are not alone, that we have never been alone, and that we will never be alone.

Jesus is our companion in the way.

In His grace, He gives me space to come to Him in my own time and in my own way. He never forces our relationship. He doesn't mind when my neediness shows up and I bray uncontrollably.

He waits.

He walks along beside.

He offers His presence.

When I demand that He be my magic genie, He gently reminds me a companion's job is not to fix everything.

A companion's job is to be there.

To journey with me.

^ ^

"The coyotes are out early tonight," Tom remarked as we finished up some yard work.

I took off my gardening gloves and listened.

"Must be ten of them out there," I replied.

A fresh kill? I wondered, shuddering at the thought.

We rarely see the coyotes who frequent our area, but we hear them regularly. Their howls and *yip-yip-yip*s reverberate through the woods and across the fields at night, causing goose bumps to tickle up my spine. Sometimes they work themselves into a frenzy, and it's hard not to guess what they're all excited about.

Coyotes normally inhabit the shadows, but on occasion they pass through the yards in our neighborhood in broad daylight:

long-legged, reddish-brown creatures preying on small rabbits and the unfortunate small cat or dog. One Christmas morning, my parents' Scottish terrier was attacked by two of them—one had the dog by the neck, the other by his haunches. The dog survived, but only because we saw what was happening and scared the coyotes off before they killed him. It was a frightening and sobering start to an otherwise festive day.

This night, we knew the coyotes were especially close to the house. Their howls rebounded off the barn and nearby tree trunks, making them sound even spookier than normal. Flash and Henry, who were standing by the fence to supervise our chores from their vantage point, turned in the direction of the noise. Ears up, nostrils wide, they were on alert that the packs were prowling.

"Glad we don't have a kitty to worry about," I said, thinking of some of the cats who had disappeared from our porch over the years.

We fell asleep that night to wide-awake coyotes, glad to be in our beds, under the blankets. I didn't think to worry about Flash and Henry.

First thing in the morning, Flash met me at the gate. He seemed jumpy, which was unusual for his low-key self. He stomped his feet and nervously bobbed his head, then turned toward Henry, who poked his nose out from behind Flash but stayed beyond my reach.

Something was wrong.

"Henry! Oh, Henderson! What happened, buddy?" I could see from his expression that he was hurt. I opened the gate and rushed to him.

That's when I saw his left ear. The tip was missing, and the tear in his raw, bleeding flesh perfectly mirrored the shape of canine teeth. "Oh NO!"

I held his ear and inspected it closely. Razor-sharp teeth marks appeared all along the jagged edge. Dear Lord, I didn't know how it was even possible to bite through something as thick and tough as a donkey ear! My dear little Henry just stared at me with incredibly sad eyes, then looked over at Flash.

"Flash, can you tell me what happened?" How I wished he could explain everything!

Hands shaking, I began to inspect both donkeys for injuries. Henry had deep scratches on both forelegs and one on the back of a hind leg. He looked like he'd just survived the worst night of his life. Flash had bloody marks on his legs and face.

There had obviously been a violent scuffle.

Coyotes.

Henry, small enough to be preyed upon, had been attacked in the middle of the night. I could only imagine how frightening it must have been!

Flash now gave Henry a nudge. *Flash must have saved him!* I thought. It was the only explanation. Henry might have been a goner if Flash had not been there to help him. Flash could have easily fought off the villains—we'd seen him in action against dogs, and believe me: You do not want to mess with him.

Thank you, God—they only got an ear.

Flash bent his head over Henry, as if to say, *I'm here for you, buddy.* Henry made a whimpering sound and looked up at him in gratitude. My heart melted. These two really *had* come a long way. Far from being indifferent to Henry, Flash was right there with him when he needed him most.

Ears forward and eyes closed, their noses touched.

Henry seemed eager for a walk, despite his injury. I cleaned the bite as best I could and then slipped his halter on in hopes that a morning stroll would help him forget the night's trauma. He started off in reverse, of course, but soon stepped along behind me, glad for the diversion. Flash followed Henry just a bit more closely than usual, and I noticed that each time we came to a stop, Flash gently groomed Henry with his teeth, scratching his back and reassuring him of his presence.

. . . for the sake of your love.

A friend of mine who recently hiked the Camino de Santiago, a five-hundred-mile pilgrimage from Saint-Jean-Pied-de-Port, France, to Santiago de Compostela, Spain, shared a prayer-poem she had meditated on many times during her long walk. My pasture was by no means the Camino, and yet the poem's words resonated with me as well:

PATIENT TRUST

Above all, trust in the slow work of God.
We are quite naturally impatient in everything
to reach the end without delay.
We should like to skip the intermediate stages.
We are impatient of being on the way to
something unknown, something new.
And yet it is the law of all progress
that it is made by passing through
some stages of instability—
and that it may take a very long time.

And so I think it is with you;
your ideas mature gradually—let them grow,
let them shape themselves, without undue haste.
Don't try to force them on,
as though you could be today what time
(that is to say, grace and circumstances
acting on your own good will)
will make of you tomorrow.

Only God could say what this new spirit
gradually forming within you will be.
Give Our Lord the benefit of believing
that his hand is leading you,
and accept the anxiety of feeling yourself
in suspense and incomplete.

Frustrated by their animosity and competitiveness, I'd been trying to push Flash and Henry to love each other. Perhaps some of that frustration was with myself for trying to force my own growth and maturity instead of letting God work according to His timetable. I was always too quick to apply a Band-Aid to every hurt, too ready with an easy answer to every question, too eager to quote a Bible verse to solve every problem. I was never comfortable with anything resembling "the slow work of God."

What we really need is patience.

We need to be okay with being "incomplete."

We need to not fear saying "I don't know."

We need to rest in God's goodness and take comfort in His companionship.

When we stop pretending we have it all together and learn to accept the instability of the in-between, what we're really doing is allowing God the freedom to slowly create us—His masterpiece—anew in Christ.

CHAPTER 13

Glory Be

Glory be to the Father,
and to the Son,
and to the Holy Ghost:
As it was in the beginning,
is now,
and ever shall be,
world without end.
Amen.

Daily Morning Prayer and Daily Evening Prayer:
Rite One, *"Gloria," The Book of Common Prayer*

stood by the back door in the kitchen and cupped my coffee mug in both hands. The cool air from outside slipped under the doorframe and across my socks; my toes curled at the chill. Through the window, I could see Flash and Henry lying down in the open barn across the pasture, their ears outlined by the barn lights shining down.

So cute.

The two were finally working out their differences well enough to sleep near each other. I imagined them talking to each other at night much the way my sister and I did when we shared a bed growing up.

"You're over the line."

"No, I'm not. You are."

"Your foot is touching me."

"No, your foot is touching me!"

"Stop breathing so loud."

"You stop breathing so loud."

I opened the door and reached for my muck boots sitting outside, shaking them in case a Texas critter had crawled inside: a spider, bug, or random snake. All clear. I slipped the boots on and tried to clomp as quietly as possible to the gate. I knew it would be impossible to sneak up on the boys, but I could try. *Goodness, I'd love to get a picture of them sleeping together . . . just once!*

As I moved the chain to open the gate, their big heads swung around and ears perked up. They didn't move again until I was halfway to the barn. Then Henry jumped up and tried to act as if he'd been standing the whole time. Flash was a little slower getting to his feet, but he, too, attempted to feign nonchalance by gazing off into the distance. *Who, me? I wasn't lying down by him; no, not me.*

"Guys, I saw you. You saw that I saw you. You can't fool me," I laughed. "Admit it; you love each other."

Flash laid his ears back and snorted at Henry, who shoe-horned his way in front to greet me. He gave Flash a shove with his back end and stuck his nose in my hand in hopes of a treat. The no-conflict zone was clearly no longer in effect, but this time I didn't get angry with them.

"Flash! Henry! I've got something for both of you." They jostled for position and gave me their best "Me first!" expressions. I pulled two animal crackers from my pocket and gave one to each. They scarfed them right down before nosing for another.

I gave them a couple more, then opened my hands to show they were empty. The donkeys eyed my hands skeptically; then Henry went for my sleeve to check for hidden treats. He nibbled the fabric with his lips, his whiskers tickling my wrist.

"Nope, none in there, silly," I laughed. He shook his mane in disappointment and gave me a clear look: *Next time, bring more.*

Scratching the top of his head, I inhaled the morning air. I loved the smell of a newborn day out here. The ground, still damp from an overnight rain, was earthy and fresh. We'd made it through another dry summer, and the ground was a thirsty sponge. Although the morning was unusually cool, it would be several weeks before "turtleneck weather" arrived, so my wrinkled neck was on its own for a while. Still, the dried pods from the mesquite trees had already fallen, and some of the oak leaves were beginning to turn. It was a hopeful sign.

^ ^

That fall, Tom and I were contracted to provide artwork and paint backdrops for a television studio in Colorado. It would be fun to collaborate on another job together—with the added pleasure of working with Bridgette and Steve, just as we had done when art was our sole business. We hired Jude (and Priscilla, his supervisor mom) to look after Flash and Henry once again.

Knowing the donkeys were in good hands, Tom and I planned to extend our trip with a short vacation at the end. We looked forward to spending a few days in the Rocky Mountains taking in the stunning fall colors. As much as I loved my big old Texas oaks and scrubby mesquites, something was drawing me to the aspens; all I wanted to do was hike to an aspen grove and sit, just *sit*, under the trees.

It wasn't easy to focus on the work to be done when vacation was on my mind. However, the physical and creative challenges of the project—faux-finishing walls and floors, installing large backdrops, creating original art—required both of us to give it our all in order to complete everything on time. It was exhausting and satisfying work, the kind we liked best.

As soon as the last piece of artwork was installed, we hit the road. Somehow we managed to catch the colors at their peak; the views were beyond spectacular. As we explored the back roads of Colorado, we spotted a grove high on a mountainside that was ablaze with color; we knew it would be the ideal spot for my aspen-sitting aspirations. I leaned forward in the passenger seat as Tom steered the rental car along winding, leaf-covered dirt roads leading us up, up, up toward our destination.

"This is it," Tom said, parking on the side of the road and pointing to a group of aspens. Up close, they were far from the thick clump of trees they appeared to be from our original vantage point. Once inside the grove, I could see they were gracefully spaced apart, with plenty of room in between for grasses and soft undergrowth. My feet nearly floated through the forest as I searched for the perfect place to spend the afternoon resting beneath the towering canopy of brilliant leaves. Tom followed, carrying a backpack filled with a blanket and picnic supplies.

The Japanese have a theory about trees. Their studies show that spending time in forests has health benefits—both mental and physical. I'd be so bold as to add "spiritual" to the list, as long as we're at it. They call it "forest bathing," but I just call it "balm for the soul." The white aspen trunks reaching upward for the deep blue sky; the shimmering leaves in yellow, green, gold, and fiery orange; a comfortable bed of grass on the forest floor . . . together creating a breathtaking, awe-inspiring cathedral.

Without realizing it, I found myself walking through the grove with arms raised and palms up to the Creator God who had made it. I loved the sound of branches touching overhead; the *ssshhh* of foliage with each puff of wind, accompanied by fresh handfuls of leafy confetti fluttering down to celebrate the changing season. It's hard to comprehend that each aspen grove, made up of hundreds of individual trees, is one *single* living organism, its roots interconnected beneath the ground.

The grove seemed to whisper to me. Inside that sanctuary

of trees, I was overwhelmed with a sense of the sacredness of this world and the beauty that beckoned my soul to worship. Though I'd brought a journal along, I couldn't bring myself to attempt to capture the feeling. Words would only fall short.

So I sat under the aspens, content to simply *be*.

∧ ∧

The drive back to Texas held another exquisite moment. While I'd been dreaming of aspens for weeks, Tom's goal was to photograph stars. In hopes of clear skies and a perfect opportunity, he planned a return route that would take us through the vast open spaces of northern New Mexico during the midnight hour. After exiting the highway in search of a farm road that was far from anywhere, we came to a stop and turned off the engine. In the darkness, there wasn't a single porch light to be found, no man-made noise to be heard.

It was so very, very dark.

So very quiet.

We looked up and gasped. Above us appeared nothing short of a stellar masterpiece: stars—by the thousands, millions.

As it was in the beginning, is now . . .

The Milky Way, in all its glory, stretched from horizon to horizon. It was so clear and close you could almost touch it, except that, as Tom explained, the closest star was about 4.3 *light-years* away. It is said that only about 9,100 stars are visible to our naked eyes, which seems like plenty until you realize you can see only the half that are in your hemisphere. That night in

New Mexico, our half—4,550 stars—was out *in force*, enchanting us, eliciting our wonder.

Tom set his camera on a tripod and pointed it at the sky. He left the aperture open for twenty seconds, long enough to let in more light than is visible to our eyes. I knew the photographs would be stunning, but I was unprepared for what showed up on the digital display screen right then and there.

My knees went weak; I was nearly light-headed. A night sky without light pollution is stunning. But a night sky without light pollution and viewed through the lens of a powerful camera? Unimaginable.

"Rachel," Tom began in a whisper, "did you know the number of stars in the observable universe is so big that it's designated with a 1 . . . with 24 zeros after it?"

"How is that even possible?" I whispered back. I shivered and pulled my coat tighter around me.

"Well, I did a little calculating," he said with a smile. "Scientists say the number of stars in the known universe is greater than the grains of sand in all the beaches and deserts in the world, which is hard to really comprehend. So I thought of another way to look at it: Picture a star as the size of a marble—a regular marble like we played with when we were kids."

"Got it."

"If each marble were to represent a star, and those marbles were spread out over the entire planet, they would need to rise to a height of more than three miles above the surface of the *entire earth*—including oceans, land, and poles—to equal the number of stars in the observable universe."

"You're making my head hurt," I laughed. I tried to imagine

flying around the world in an airplane, looking down at an unending landscape of multicolored marbles as far as I could see and deeper than I could fathom.

"Each time astronomers are able to look farther and farther out into space, they see more galaxies and more stars. Astronomers working with the Hubble Space Telescope picked the darkest spot in space they could find—about the size of what you'd see at the end of an eight-foot drinking straw. They focused the telescope on that spot for eleven days because they were curious about what they would find."

"And?" I didn't know where this was leading, but I sensed my science-loving husband was about to unload a doozy of a fact right there in the middle of nowhere.

"They found that just in that tiny little dark spot there are ten thousand points of light. Each of those points of light is a galaxy, and each galaxy contains at least one hundred billion stars."

"That's just not possible," I said, not whispering anymore.

"I know it's hard to believe, but it's absolutely true," he said. "And it takes so long for the light to travel to us that, in a very real sense, we're looking into the past when we look at stars." Tom shook his head as he let it sink in for himself, then looked at me through the darkness. "We mere humans have no idea what we're doing."

Feeling like unimaginably tiny creatures on a small planet, in a single solar system, inside an average-sized galaxy 2.5 million *light-years* from Andromeda (our nearest galaxy), and within a known universe of 2 *trillion* galaxies, we stood there with faces upturned, trying—unsuccessfully—to take it all in.

^ ^

Still reeling from the beauty of the aspen grove in Colorado and the intensity of northern New Mexico's night sky, my first few days back in Texas blurred by. It had done me such good to step away from my everyday life and take time for wonder.

Researchers say that awe sharpens your brain, and I do not doubt it for one moment. Something happens when you encounter indescribable beauty, or witness the incredible forces of nature, or see landscapes that make you weep. We become aware of our smallness—our ephemeral existence on this earth—and suddenly it only makes sense to jettison the petty matters occupying our thoughts and wasting our energies. We become aware that God is bigger than any construct we can make, and we know in our hearts He cannot be adequately described by any system—scientific or theological—that our human brains can devise.

We become aware of the God who simply *is*.

We become aware of the God in whom, as Paul said, "we live and move and have our being"—*our very being*.

I found an old stump at the edge of the pasture so I could try explaining this to Henry, who seemed to have more time than Flash to listen to my musings. I barely had a chance to set his halter on the ground and sit down before he was backing into my lap, nearly knocking me off. It wasn't the best arrangement for a conversation, but it would have to do.

I began to scratch him with both hands, and he looked over his shoulder with deep appreciation. "You owe me, Henry," I scolded him. He twitched his ears in reply. Then, as if to make up for it, he turned his whole body and put his head right on

205

my chest. With a little sigh, he looked up at me with those soulful eyes, relaxed the weight of his head into my arms, and snuggled in close.

"Oh, Henderson Number Ten," I murmured into his ear. "I love you." I ran my hands down his neck to tousle his bristly mane, then watched it pop right back up.

This little guy.

I had thought Henry would be my "happily ever after" donkey. I'd wanted him to fix my dreadful mistake, trying to force him to make up for Penny and Prince. I'd hoped he would be Flash's wingman. I had wanted him to be good, to be quiet, and to behave.

But Henry had refused to cooperate with my agenda. He'd come on his own terms, making me accept him and love him for who he is, not for who I wanted him to be. There was never any pretense with him. He's the same on the outside as he is on the inside: a congruent donkey.

I still have a lot to learn from him.

Here he was with his notched ear and scrappy personality, simply wanting to be noticed and loved. How could I not just adore him? I stroked his dark coat, which was getting thicker with the cooler temperatures. He blinked and moved his fuzzy lips, as if trying to tell me something. That he was happy to be right where he was?

I was thinking the same thing, Henry.

I'd missed my walks with Henry while we were gone. He was understandably more interested in being massaged than in walking, but I wanted to resume my pasture prayer practice and was hoping to persuade him to go for an amble on the paths. By now I no longer needed my notebook; the Creeds and my favorite psalms and prayers were deep in my heart, a ready liturgy for impromptu meditation.

With an indulgent expression, Flash watched us—

Henry standing still for his halter.

My gentle tug on the rope: "Walk on, Henry! Walk on!"

Henry's progression from a backward stance to starting position: first taking time to mull it over; then his slow turn forward; and finally . . . moving ahead with a *phhh* over his shoulder that said, *Hey, Flash, come along!*

Flash didn't need a prompt. Ears up and tail swaying, he fell into line and brought up the rear. These days, I couldn't get one donkey without the other. They were always together. I guess they'd become each other's wingman after all.

Glory be . . .

The simple pleasure of walking with donkeys is never lost on me: Henry alongside, his mane ruffling in the wind and nostrils in constant motion; Flash plodding behind us, content to follow. On our beloved trail we went, around the pasture at the pace of Henry's sturdy legs.

With these donkeys, I had traveled through time to meet biblical characters—even Jesus Himself. They were touchpoints that allowed me to step into the pages of history and immerse myself in the stories ancient donkeys had helped shape. Scripture began to live again for me because I was seeing it with new eyes. Henry's arrival, too, had invited me out of the boxes I'd lived in for a long time and into the expanse of creation. There I encountered the beauty of mystery and faith as we both let down our guards, became open to change, and were willing to trust.

Henry paused to make sure Flash was still with us. I took advantage of the moment to breathe the words of the "Gloria" doxology once again. This path had paved a way for new forms of prayer to revive my tired soul. When I had run out of words and was running on spiritual fumes, liturgy and spiritual practice had put enough wind back into my sails to propel me forward without the fear I would lose my way in the process. I could embark on another season of life knowing God would be with me. I was especially thankful for this little donkey who had taught me so much about trusting God with this sacred journey.

What a gift you are, Henry.

"May I join you?" Tom met Henry and me at the barn as we approached from the trail around the north pasture. Flash had peeled off from our excursion before the finish line, distracted by a new patch of grass that had sprung up. Henry hadn't yet noticed Flash's fadeaway and now looked eagerly at Tom, who held a cup of fresh coffee in his hands.

"I think we're done walking for today, but I'd love to sit out here with you," I said, eyeing the coffee while I removed Henry's halter. "It's too nice to be inside!"

It's always a good sign when your non-coffee-drinking husband holds a steaming cup of brew—it means you're about to receive a delicious gift, made just the way you like it.

"I was hoping you'd say that," he said with a smile, handing the mug to me. "I've got camp chairs set up by the firepit."

We settled into the canvas chairs and propped our feet on the stones that circled the firepit just outside the barn. Even without a fire, the setting put us both in contemplative moods.

Our time in the mountains had profoundly affected both of us, and it was difficult to articulate its impact.

Henry lingered nearby, his ears flicking toward us as if trying to eavesdrop on our quiet conversation. He was probably waiting to see if any sweet coffee would be left in my cup—a treat he was known to lick up when the opportunity presented itself.

After sitting in silence for a while, Tom posed what seemed like a random question: "Rachel, what do you think God looks like?"

Tears immediately stung my eyes. I didn't know why.

I blinked hard and stammered something about how nobody really knows, and that it's silly to try to imagine—He's just too big. I smoothed my jeans and fiddled with a loose seam on the armrest to avoid answering. *This is what my whole journey has been about, hasn't it?*

"I'm not trying to be clever. I just wonder," he said. "I wonder what God is like. I mean, if you were to close your eyes and imagine standing in front of Him, what do you think He would look like?"

I protested again.

And then I took a breath and closed my eyes.

They couldn't have been shut for more than a few seconds.

But I saw something. *Felt something.*

I can't say it was a vision; I wouldn't feel comfortable making that kind of claim. All I know is what my mind saw, in that moment, on a cool autumn afternoon.

I saw what I saw.

I had closed my eyes, and people, places, landscapes—the world—rushed past me like a wave going out to sea. In a moment, I found myself in a serene valley, with hills gently rising on both sides. The sky was deep azure, like no other blue I had ever seen, and I stood beneath it in tall, silvery grass that swayed in a barely perceptible breeze.

And He was there.

He was there in front of me—a brilliant, beautiful mass of light. White light at the center radiated out, and like a prism, it became the colors of the rainbow at the edges. The aura seemed to float above the ground, and I looked right at it, right into the middle. It was warm and beautiful, and utterly, completely captivating.

I knew instantly, without thinking, that this Light was God's real presence with me.

I was immersed in it, bathed in a fine mist of glimmering particles.

Its rays swept round me, as if examining the very inside of me—my heart, my mind, everything. No warning, no chance to get my thoughts in order, no way to make things presentable, no possibility of propping things up . . . but it didn't matter.

It lasted only a few seconds, maybe four, maybe five, but it was as if the Light had scanned my entire life. All of it.

It happened so fast.

Me as a child—gawky and unsure of myself. The times I cheated on my third-grade math tests. My hunger for approval as a teenager. My fears of missing out. My anxieties as a mom. The times I failed people I loved. The lost baby, the disappointments, the struggles through the recession, my worries about the future, my doubts and questions about God. Me, trying to have it all together and falling short.

All the things I've done.

What I've left undone.

Penny and Prince.

My walks and my loneliness, my hopes and my dreams.

The Light saw me—all of me—and knew me.

I was known. Completely known.

I was in the Light . . . and I was not one bit embarrassed or ashamed.

I surrendered to what felt like a powerful wave, my toes leaving the sand as the water closed over me.

Yet I was not afraid. In my deepest, worst fear of drowning, I found I could breathe. I was breathing.

This is love. *This* is love.

This is love.

Abruptly, I opened my eyes. The Light disappeared, and tears streamed down my face.

It was too beautiful, too lovely, too perfect to bear. I couldn't say anything.

Because I knew.

I saw Light, and I saw Love. It had pulled me under, but instead of drowning, I breathed Him in and found life.

And I knew—this is who God is.

God is love.

God is . . . *love.*

Sitting in a camp chair near a little chocolate-brown donkey, on a cool autumn afternoon, I know what I saw. I cannot explain it, cannot describe it, cannot even fathom it; but somehow it changed me.

It had made me feel whole.

And I've come to realize this is what Love does.

It sees all and loves all.

It cannot do anything but that.

Love only asks us to let go. It asks us to let go of the past that holds us in regret and guilt. It asks us to let go of our need to control the present. It asks us to let go of our anxieties about the future. It asks us to let go of our fear of never being enough, our fear of not having all the right answers, and our fear that God is anything less than merciful, compassionate, and full of grace.

In asking us to let go, Love—God Himself—in turn assures us that our broken pieces will be restored.

All shall be made right.

Everything is going to be okay.

No matter where our journey takes us, we never walk alone.

Your Guide to Prayer Walking

Incorporating liturgy and written prayers into time spent outdoors has transformed my spiritual life. Now, I do realize not everyone shares my unique situation: I have a couple of special donkeys, as well as access to a secluded pasture with walking paths. But I believe that anyone can benefit from the principles of prayer walking, no matter where you find yourself. Whether you live in a city or in suburbia or in the countryside, it's good for your soul to step beyond your living room and breathe outside air, giving your heart and mind a chance to settle into a rhythm of prayer.

For me, finding (or creating) a daily liturgy makes this kind of prayer possible. On the following page, I've listed several prayers and readings that I use—some from online versions of *The Book of Common Prayer*, and others that I've discovered elsewhere. The liturgy example found in Brian Zahnd's book *Water to Wine* is also a wonderful place to start! It helped me realize I have the freedom to combine liturgical prayers and Creeds with my own personal prayers. Having access to these resources via a link on my phone or a notes app is a modern convenience I embrace. I have also used a pocket-sized note-book for keeping my favorite prayers handy.

This is the order I typically use if I'm not following a pre-scribed Daily Office:

Salutation/*Gloria*
Opening Verse
The Jesus Prayer
Confession of Sin
Apostles' Creed
Psalm or Verse (I love Psalm 23 here.)
The Lord's Prayer
Personal Prayers
Prayer of General Thanksgiving
Prayer for the Week
Prayer for Mission
Confession of the Mystery
The Jesus Prayer
Amen

See how my personal prayers—for my family, friends, and circumstances—are tucked in there? All the rest, with the exception of the Prayer for the Week, I have memorized through simple repetition and by writing them out. The online versions of The Daily Offices also offer additional Scripture readings and prayers—they can be done later (when I'm not walking and prone to trip) or if I choose to pray indoors that day.

If you're interested in incorporating set prayers into your prayer walk, may I suggest the following tips?

1. **Establish a regular walking route.** Walking the same patterns with regularity will allow your mind to settle into a rhythm. You won't need to think about which way to go next or wonder how long it will take you.

2. **Try associating certain landmarks with particular prayers.** For example, as I approach the pasture gate, I simply pray, "Lord, open my lips and my mouth shall proclaim your praise. Glory be to the Father, and to the Son, and to the Holy Ghost: As it was in the beginning, is now, and ever shall be, world without end. Amen." Here I combine a salutation (an opening direct address to God) with the *Gloria.* As I open the gate, I begin The Confession of Sin. The routine helps me remember the order of the prayers and has the added benefit of bringing the prayers to mind whenever I happen by that location at other times.

3. **Keep it simple.** Work on committing one prayer to memory at a time. I spent weeks on The Prayer of General Thanksgiving, offering it to the Lord over and over again. Sometimes it was the only prayer I read that day. Over time, it became a dear friend! Now when I see it pop up daily in *The Book of Common Prayer,* I don't have to read it. I can simply breathe it, lingering on the words and phrases. It never gets old.

4. **Don't worry about the repetition.** I grew up worried about falling into "vain repetitions" in my prayers. Yet my "free-form" prayers were every bit as repetitious as the liturgical ones, except not nearly as full of beautiful theology and form. "Lord, I just ask . . ." is the liturgy of my former prayer

life. Accessing the deep wells of Christian traditional prayers broadens the language and scope of my prayers. Rather than praying mostly for "me and my needs," liturgical prayers are often "we and us" focused. I'm reminded I'm praying the same prayers as millions of other Christians around the world—past, present, *and* future. We are part of a collective prayer stream that carries and sustains the faithful. What a beautiful thought . . .

5. **Change things up if you need to.** Summers in Texas are HOT, y'all! I don't like to sweat. My living room couch provides a very good alternative for those days I just can't bear the heat outside. I also don't like extreme cold or other inclement weather, so I gravitate to my couch during those times as well.

6. **Make space for silence.** When it comes to prayer, don't feel the need to do all the talking. Embrace quiet. Experience wonder. Notice the grass, the trees, the wind, the sky. Pay attention to your surroundings. Set your anxieties aside. Oftentimes, wisdom arrives through observation. You can better hear God directing your thoughts and speaking to your heart when you make more room for Him to do so.

7. **Don't look for "results"; be at peace with the simple practice of prayer.** I realized that often in the past, I'd been steeped in results-oriented prayer. I viewed prayer as a "battle"—something that would persuade God to do what I wanted (or felt I needed) Him to do. True, Jesus said we should bring our requests and desires to Him. We should intercede for others' needs. But we can also rest in the knowledge that God knows what we need before we even ask, and He is able to answer in His own way, in His own time. There

is no need to coerce or entice Him to see things our way. Prayer as the practice of being in God's presence—through quiet meditation on Scripture and liturgy and silent listening with an attitude of trust—is transformative and powerful.

8. **Journey forward in humility and honesty.** Forming new habits such as prayer walking takes time. Have patience with the process and realize you'll never be an "expert" at prayer and the spiritual life. I certainly am not. But when we venture forward with the desire to grow, to mature, to leave behind easy answers and old ways, it will require us to ask for help along the way. We must understand there is much to be learned from others who may come from another denomination or faith stream. Be a learner—read widely and look willingly at the other side of the coin. And in the process, don't be afraid to say, "I don't know." Trust that God is with you, even in the unknowing.

9. **You can find the prayers listed on page 214 written out at www.rachelanneridge.com/liturgy.**

Acknowledgments

It takes a team of people to transform an idea into a published book, and I'm grateful to "Team Henry" at Tyndale House Publishers for your enthusiasm and heart for this one! Sarah Atkinson, your vision for *Walking with Henry* helped me stay true to the story. Bonne Steffen, my dear editor, you made this process fun and practically pain-free! You are a delight to work with, and I appreciate how you polish my words until they gleam. Anisa Baker in editorial and Kara Leonino and Jillian Schlossberg in acquisitions—you are all amazing. Thank you, Libby Dykstra, for your incredible design; Kristen Magnesen in marketing and Mariah Franklin in public relations for your fresh strategies and tireless pitches to create buzz about the book; and Nate Rische and Jennifer Schindler in production for keeping the book on track and ensuring it's printed "just so." I am grateful to each of you.

There are many other special people who were instrumental in my life as I wrote this book; here are shout-outs to a few of them:

Rev. Walt Marcum: Thank you for teaching seminary-level courses during the Kerygma service each Sunday morning at HPUMC. You've made Jesus, the Bible, church history, and science and faith come alive in new ways for both Tom and me.

Rev. Barbara Marcum: You were my first female pastor, the one who made me say, "Oh, I get it now!" Thank you for your kindness, grace-filled presence, and ministry.

Jack Levison: I didn't discover your insight about Jesus being with wild beasts during his forty-day temptation in the wilderness until after my manuscript was written; I found it eye opening and too good to not include parts of it:

> Jesus had to leave behind this remarkable experience [his baptism with the Holy Spirit] on the banks of the Jordan River in order to exercise his vocation and to grasp, ultimately, God's commitment to him. The simple detail that Jesus was "with the wild animals" points to this [see Mark 1:13]. Typically, wild animals were seen as a threat, as in Psalm 22:11-21 and Ezekiel 34:8. Mark, however, uses simple grammar: "he was with," which indicates peaceful coexistence (Mark 3:14, 5:18, 14:67). Jesus coexisted peacefully with wild animals. The usual hostility between human and beast is gone. Jesus, in essence, reestablishes a forty-day epoch of Eden, when the animals live peaceably with human beings.
>
> The simple detail that Jesus coexisted with the animals fulfills all sorts of Israelite hopes for a restoration of Eden, for a return to a peaceful coexistence with wild beasts.[1]

Priscilla Pope-Levison: Thank you for introducing me to Benedictine prayer and encouraging my prayer practices. You wisely explained, "We have these prayers that people think are just rote prayers, but they are formative, and they are forming us even when we aren't thinking about them. They become internalized and become part of who we are." One conversation over tacos with a professor I admired led to friendship and so much more.

Peri Zahnd: "Write the book that's in your heart," you said to me. I cherished your words, and your encouragement helped me be unafraid.

---

[1] Jack Levison, *Fresh Air: The Holy Spirit for an Inspired Life* (Brewster, MA: Paraclete, 2012), 175.

Brian Zahnd: Your saying that "God is like Jesus. God has always been like Jesus. There has never been a time when God was not like Jesus. We have not always known what God is like—but now we do"[2] is one of the best things I've ever heard.

Ruth Samsel: Thank you for your tireless efforts and your fountain of ideas for my work. You will always hold a special place in my heart as my agent and friend.

My parents, Tom and Anne Rasmussen: You've prayed for me every single day of my life. How I treasure that! I am so thankful for your love, for your lives, and for introducing me to Jesus.

My firstborn, Lauren: Your wellness journey over this past year has inspired me to be more honest and open with my own struggles (and victories), and it's made all the difference in writing this book.

All my kids and their spouses and children—Lauren and Robert, Meghan and Nathan, and Grayson and Emily: Honestly, I hit the mother lode with all of you! Ivy, Heidi, Hazel, August, and Caroline: Being your nana is the best thing ever. I can't wait for our next sleepover!

Tommy: This journey has only been possible because of your love, companionship, and support. You've made our life together an adventure, and I love you more than ever.

Finally, Henry: I'm so grateful Doc Darrin spotted your fuzzy ears in a sea of a thousand donkeys. The grace that brought you to me is the same grace that leads *me* home.

[2] Brian Zahnd, "God Is like Jesus," August 11, 2011, https://brianzahnd.com/2011/08/god-is-like-jesus-2/.

Notes

CHAPTER 1: THE MEANS OF GRACE

8 *"I have discovered that something is awakened . . ."* Makoto Fujimura, *Culture Care: Reconnecting with Beauty for Our Common Life* (Downers Grove, IL: InterVarsity Press, 2017), 4.

10 *"his descendants would number as countless as the stars."* See Genesis 15:5.

CHAPTER 2: I BELIEVE

28 *"His invitation—'Follow Me!'"* See Matthew 9:9, NASB.

28 *"No wonder His disciples risked everything to be known as people of 'the Way.'"* See Acts 9:2.

28 *"Hammered out in AD 325 . . ."* See JoHannah Reardon, "The Nicene and Apostles' Creeds," *Christianity Today*, July 30, 2008, http://www .christianitytoday.com/biblestudies/articles/churchhomeleadership /nicene-apostles-creeds.html.

CHAPTER 3: ALL THAT I NEED

37 *"I was implementing the 'KonMari' method . . ."* See "KonMari: How to Clean Up Your Home Once and Never Need to Do It Again," Martha Stewart, March 20, 2015, https://www.marthastewart.com/1106009 /konmari-trendy-new-organizing-method.

CHAPTER 4: OPEN OUR EYES

58 *"'I do not believe that the God who created all the universe . . .'"* Francis S. Collins, *The Language of God: A Scientist Presents Evidence for Belief* (New York: Free Press, 2006), 210.

60 *"I'm happy to report that donkeys made the list!"* Job 39:5-8 is part of God's response to Job: "Who gives the wild donkey its freedom? Who untied its ropes? I have placed it in the wilderness; its home is the wasteland. It

hates the noise of the city and has no driver to shout at it. The mountains
are its pastureland, where it searches for every blade of grass."
61   *"Don't be afraid,' Jesus said."* See Matthew 14:27.

CHAPTER 5: WHAT WE'VE LEFT UNDONE
77   *"'come boldly before the throne' and 'claim the promises.'"* See Hebrews 4:16
and 2 Peter 1:4.
78   *"Did you know that His mercies never end—they are new every morning?"*
See Lamentations 3:22-23.

CHAPTER 6: THIS NEW DAY
91   *"Liturgy is literally 'a work of the people,' or even better, 'a work* for *the
people.'"* See "Liturgy, 'The Work of the People'? Or Not?" Episcopal
Café, September 29, 2011, https://www.episcopalcafe.com/liturgy_the
_work_of_the_people_or_not/.

CHAPTER 7: PEOPLE OF HIS PASTURE
102   *"The ever-changing sky was a solid dome . . ."* See Paul H. Seely, "The
Firmament and the Water Above," *Westminster Theological Journal* 53
(1991): 227–40, http://faculty.gordon.edu/hu/bi/ted_hildebrandt
/OTeSources/01-Genesis/Text/Articles-Books/Seely-Firmament-WTJ.pdf.
105   *"I'd pulled* The Big Book of Bible Difficulties . . ." See Norman L. Geisler
and Thomas Howe, *The Big Book of Bible Difficulties* (Grand Rapids, MI:
Baker Books, 2008).
106   *"'Most of us are probably unprepared . . .'"* John H. Walton and D. Brent
Sandy, *The Lost World of Scripture: Ancient Literary Culture and Biblical
Authority* (Downers Grove, IL: IVP Academic, 2013), 13.
110–11   *"'God must be present in every single creature . . .'"* Martin Luther, *The
Annotated Luther, Vol. 3: Church and Sacraments*, Paul W. Robinson, ed.
(Minneapolis: Fortress Press, 2016), 205.
111   *"'animals are designated as footprints of God.'"* Jaroslav Pelikan, ed., *Luther's
Works*, vol. 1, *Lectures on Genesis, Chapters 1–5* (St. Louis: Concordia,
1958), 68.

CHAPTER 8: LEAD US NOT
126   *"'When you pray, say this . . .'"* See Matthew 6:7-13.
126   *"'Maybe you can't even remember the last time . . .'"* Don Underwood,
Pray Like Jesus: Rediscovering the Lord's Prayer (Nashville: Abingdon Press,
2017), 10.
128   *"'Faith never knows where it is being led . . .'"* Oswald Chambers, *My
Utmost for His Highest*, March 19, accessed August 7, 2018, https://
utmost.org/classic/the-way-of-abraham-in-faith-classic/.
131   *"'He made from one man every nation . . .'"* Acts 17:26-27, ESV

CHAPTER 9: INFECTED HEARTS

143 *"'The gulf that exists between us as people . . .'"* From the foreword, *All These Wonders: True Stories about Facing the Unknown*, Catherine Burns, ed. (New York: Crown Archetype, 2017), xiii.

149 *"One day an expert in religious law stood up . . ."* Luke 10:25-29.

149–51 *"A Jewish man was traveling from Jerusalem to Jericho . . ."* Paraphrased from Luke 10:30-37.

CHAPTER 10: O GRACIOUS LIGHT

156 *"The descending light danced to the whirring hum of cicadas . . ."* The cicadas' mating call is an acoustical wonder. See "Secrets of the Cicada's Sound," ScienceDaily, May 20, 2013, https://www.sciencedaily.com /releases/2013/05/130530152846.htm.

158 *"it's one of the oldest forms of spiritual discipline . . ."* "Fixed-hour prayer is the oldest form of Christian spiritual discipline and has its roots in the Judaism out of which Christianity came. When the Psalmist says, 'Seven times a day do I praise You,' he is referring to fixed-hour prayer as it existed in ancient Judaism. We do not know the hours that were appointed in the Psalmist's time for those prayers. By the turn of the era, however, the devout had come to punctuate their work day with prayers on a regimen that followed the flow of Roman commercial life." The Works of Phyllis Tickle, "About Fixed-Hour Prayer," accessed August 10, 2018, http://www.phyllistickle.com/fixed-hour-prayer/.

158 *"pray without ceasing"* 1 Thessalonians 5:17, KJV.

160 *"'Joyous light of glory of the immortal Father . . .'"* *Wikipedia*, s.v. "Phos Hilaron," last modified July 13, 2018, https://en.wikipedia.org/wiki /Phos_Hilaron.

166–67 *"They become particles or they become waves depending on whether they are being observed."* See Weizmann Institute of Science, "Quantum Theory Demonstrated: Observation Affects Reality," ScienceDaily, February 27, 1998, https://www.sciencedaily.com/releases/1998/02/980227055013 .htm.

167 *"'If you know where an electron is . . .'"* Barbara Brown Taylor, *The Luminous Web: Essays on Science and Religion* (Lanham, MD: Rowman & Littlefield, 2000), 50.

167 *"'the true Light . . . coming into the world . . . that illumines every person'"* John 1:9, AMPC.

168 *"'There is a crack in everything / That's how the light gets in.'"* Leonard Cohen, "Anthem," 1992, copyright © Sony/ATV Music Publishing (UK) Limited.

168 *"'You cause them to drink . . .'"* Psalm 36:8-9, AMPC.

CHAPTER 11: THE WAY OF PEACE

174 *"It's not exactly clear since Matthew's account differs from the other Gospels."*
Matthew 21:2-3, 7 mentions two animals—a donkey and a colt; Mark
11:2-7 and Luke 19:30-35 record only a young donkey; and John 12:14
says that "Jesus found a young donkey and rode on it."

174 *"the crowds must have immediately thought of Zechariah's Old Testament
prophecy . . ."* See Zechariah 9:9.

177 *"The Christian life is the lifelong practice of attending to the details
of congruence . . ."* Eugene Peterson, *As Kingfishers Catch Fire:
A Conversation on the Ways of God Formed by the Words of God*
(New York: WaterBrook, 2017), xviii.

178 *"a beauty that will save the world."* Brian Zahnd, *Beauty Will Save the
World: Rediscovering the Allure and Mystery of Christianity* (Lake Mary, FL:
Charisma House, 2012), 225.

CHAPTER 12: COMPANION IN THE WAY

189 *"It's a book of prayers . . ."* See John Baillie, *A Diary of Private Prayer*
(New York: Scribner, 2014 ed.).

193 *"A friend of mine who recently hiked the Camino de Santiago . . ."* My
friend Peri Zahnd documented his journey in *Every Scene By Heart:
A Camino de Santiago Memoir*, St. Joseph, MO: Spello Press, 2017.

193–94 "Patient Trust," by Pierre Teilhard de Chardin, included in *Hearts on
Fire: Praying with Jesuits*, ed. Michael Harter, SJ (Chicago: Loyola,
2005), 102–3.

195 *"allowing God the freedom to slowly create us—His masterpiece—anew in
Christ."* See Ephesians 2:10.

CHAPTER 13: GLORY BE

201 *"They call it 'forest bathing' . . ."* See Ephrat Livini, "The Japanese Practice
of 'Forest Bathing' Is Scientifically Proven to Be Good for You," World
Economic Forum (in collaboration with *Quartz*), March 23, 2017,
https://www.weforum.org/agenda/2017/03/the-japanese-practice-of
-forest-bathing-is-scientifically-proven-to-be-good-for-you.

201 *"It's hard to comprehend that each aspen grove . . ."* See Anna Norris, "The
Secret Lives of Aspen Groves," The Weather Channel, November 19,
2015, https://weather.com/science/nature/news/secret-life-aspen-groves.

202 *"The Milky Way, in all its glory . . ."* See Tim Sharp, "Alpha Centauri:
Nearest Star System to the Sun," SPACE.com, January 18, 2018, https://
www.space.com/18090-alpha-centauri-nearest-star-system.html; and
Bob King, "9,096 Stars in the Sky—Is That All?" *Sky & Telescope*,
September 17, 2014, https://www.skyandtelescope.com/astronomy
-resources/how-many-stars-night-sky-09172014/.

204 *"Each time astronomers are able to look farther and farther out into space . . ."*
See "Hubble Sees Galaxies Galore," Hubble Space Telescope, accessed
August 23, 2018, https://www.spacetelescope.org/images/heic0406a/;
"Hubble Digs Deeply, Toward Big Bang," NASA, March 9, 2004, https://
www.nasa.gov/vision/universe/starsgalaxies/hubble_UDF.html; and
Elizabeth Howell, "How Many Stars Are in the Universe?" SPACE.com,
May 17, 2017, https://www.space.com/26078-how-many-stars-are-there
.html.

205 *"Researchers say that awe sharpens your brain . . ."* See Michelle Lani
Shiota, "How Awe Sharpens Our Brains," *Greater Good Magazine*,
May 11, 2016, https://greatergood.berkeley.edu/article/item/how
_awe_sharpens_our_brains.

205 *"we live and move and have our being."* Acts 17:28, NIV.

Resources

Liturgies/Prayer

Baillie, John. *A Diary of Private Prayer*. Updated and revised by Susanna Wright. New York: Scribner, 2014.

The Book of Common Prayer. An online version of TBOCP can be accessed at http://www.bookofcommonprayer.net/ (select "Daily Offices" at the top and then "Today's Office" in the drop-down menu); The Daily Office can be accessed at https://gregorians.org/office/ and also through a variety of apps available for iPhone and Android users.

Brueggemann, Walter. *A Way Other than Our Own: Devotions for Lent*. Louisville: Westminster John Knox, 2017.

Butcher, Carmen Acevedo, trans. *The Cloud of Unknowing*. Boston: Shambhala, 2009. (explores how early Christians thought of prayer)

Claiborne, Shane, Jonathan Wilson-Hartgrove, and Enuma Okoro. *Common Prayer: A Liturgy for Ordinary Radicals*. Grand Rapids, MI: Zondervan, 2010.

Cyzewski, Ed. *Flee, Be Silent, Pray: An Anxious Evangelical Finds Peace with God through Contemplative Prayer*. Self-published, 2017.

Marshall, Catherine. *The Prayers of Peter Marshall*. New York: McGraw-Hill, 1954.

McKelvey, Douglas. *Every Moment Holy*. Nashville: Rabbit Room, 2017.

Tickle, Phyllis. *The Divine Hours: A Manual for Prayer* (three seasonal volumes for the calendar year). New York: Image Books, 2006. (An online version of The Divine Hours can be accessed at http:// annarborvineyard.org/tdh/tdh.cfm.)

Warren, Tish Harrison. *Liturgy of the Ordinary: Sacred Practices in Everyday Life*. Downers Grove, IL: IVP Books, 2016.

Spiritual Practice

Blanksi, Tyler. *When Donkeys Talk: A Quest to Rediscover the Mystery and Wonder of Christianity.* Grand Rapids, MI: Zondervan, 2013.

Calhoun, Adele Ahlberg. *Spiritual Disciplines Handbook: Practices That Transform Us*. Downers Grove, IL: IVP Books, 2015.

Chole, Alicia Britt. *The Sacred Slow: A Holy Departure from Fast Faith*. Nashville: W Publishing, 2017.

Levison, Jack. *40 Days with the Holy Spirit: Fresh Air for Every Day*. Brewster, MA: Paraclete, 2015.

Packiam, Glenn. *Discover the Mystery of Faith: How Worship Shapes Believing*. Colorado Springs: David C Cook, 2013.

Smith, James K. A. *You Are What You Love: The Spiritual Power of Habit*. Grand Rapids, MI: Brazos, 2016.

Smith, Traci. *Faithful Families: Creating Sacred Moments at Home.* St. Louis: Chalice, 2017.

Ware, Bishop Kallistos. *The Orthodox Way.* Crestwood, NY: St. Vladimir's Seminary Press, 1995.

Webber, Robert, and Lester Ruth. *Evangelicals on the Canterbury Trail: Why Evangelicals Are Attracted to the Liturgical Church* (rev. ed.). New York: Morehouse, 2013.

Willard, Dallas. *The Divine Conspiracy: Rediscovering Our Hidden Life in God.* San Francisco: HarperSanFrancisco, 1998.

Zahnd, Brian. *Water to Wine: Some of My Story.* St. Joseph, MO: Spello, 2016. (Liturgy is found in chapter 4 on prayer.)

Bible/Church History

Hart, David Bentley. *The Story of Christianity: An Illustrated History of 2000 Years of the Christian Faith.* New York: Quercus, 2012.

Marcum, Rev. Walt. Sermon series on church history. 2016–2017. http://www.hpumc.org/sermon-library/kerygma-sermons/.

Wilken, Robert Louis. *The First Thousand Years: A Global History of Christianity.* New Haven, CT: Yale University Press, 2012.

Wright, N. T. *The Challenge of Jesus: Rediscovering Who Jesus Was and Is.* Downers Grove, IL: InterVarsity, 2015.

Wright, N. T. *Simply Jesus: A New Vision of Who He Was, What He Did, And Why He Matters.* New York: HarperOne, 2018.

Faith/Science

BioLogos. https://biologos.org. "BioLogos invites the church and the world to see the harmony between science and biblical faith as we present an evolutionary understanding of God's creation."

Collins, Francis S. *The Language of God: A Scientist Presents Evidence for Belief.* New York: Free Press, 2007.

Copan, Paul, Tremper Longman III, Christopher L. Reese, and Michael G. Strauss, eds. *Dictionary of Christianity and Science: The Definitive Reference for the Intersection of Christian Faith and Contemporary Science.* Grand Rapids, MI: Zondervan, 2017.

Polkinghorne, John. *Quantum Physics and Theology: An Unexpected Kinship.* New Haven, CT: Yale University Press, 2008.

Walton, John H. *Genesis 1 as Ancient Cosmology.* University Park, PA: Penn State University Press, 2011.

Walton, John H. *The Lost World of Genesis One: Ancient Cosmology and the Origins Debate.* Downers Grove, IL: IVP Academic, 2009.

Young, Davis A., and Ralph F. Stearley. *The Bible, Rocks and Time: Geological Evidence for the Age of the Earth.* Downers Grove, IL: IVP Academic, 2008.

About the Author
(and Her Donkeys)

Rachel Anne Ridge is an artist, a writer, and a stray donkey rescuer who lives in Texas. Together with her husband, Tom, she raised three kids, bootstrapped her way through the Great Recession, and rediscovered God amid the everyday juggle of life. Through her writing and online presence at rachelanneridge.com, she helps people around the world find beauty and faith in the unexpected and often unappreciated moments that life brings. Rachel's books—*Flash: The Homeless Donkey Who Taught Me about Life, Faith, and Second Chances* and *Walking with Henry: Big Lessons from a Little Donkey on Faith, Friendship, and Finding*

Your Path—reveal how God uses ordinary, sometimes humorous means to help us see Him—and to change our lives forever.

Henry the Donkey is outgoing and friendly, and he loves being around people. He enjoys rolling in the dirt, scratching against fence posts, and napping in the sun. Henry's favorite snack is animal crackers, and he's been known to do yoga when he thinks no one is watching.

Flash the Donkey approaches life with curiosity and hopefulness. He always wants to know what everyone is doing, and he is forever optimistic that carrots will be involved. He enjoys spending time with his friend Henry and is happiest in a field of yellow wildflowers.

The heartwarming true tale of an
irrepressible donkey who needed a home—
and forever changed a family.

978-1-4143-9783-2 (Hardcover)
978-1-4143-9784-9 (Softcover)

When Rachel Anne Ridge discovered a wounded, frightened donkey standing in her driveway, she couldn't turn
him away. And against all odds, he turned out to be the
very thing her family needed most. They let him into their
hearts . . . and he taught them things they never knew
about life, love, and faith.

Prepare to fall in love with Flash: a quirky, unlikely hero
with gigantic ears, a deafening bray, a personality as big
as Texas, and a story you'll never forget.

Available everywhere books are sold.

CP0850

FLASH CONTINUES HIS ADVENTURES WITH YOUNG READERS . . .

FLASH THE DONKEY
Makes New Friends

Written and Illustrated by

RACHEL ANNE RIDGE

978-1-4964-1395-6

Inspired by Rachel Anne Ridge's memoir *Flash: The Homeless Donkey Who Taught Me about Life, Faith, and Second Chances,* children will fall in love with this endearing donkey as he and his friends learn to appreciate the values of working together and true friendship.

CP1127